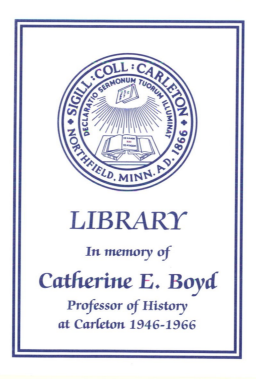

Growing Up Palestinian

Growing Up Palestinian
ISRAELI OCCUPATION AND
THE INTIFADA GENERATION

Laetitia Bucaille

Translated by Anthony Roberts

PRINCETON UNIVERSITY PRESS

PRINCETON AND OXFORD

First published in French under the title *Générations Intifada,* © Hachette Littératures 2002

Copyright © 2004 by Princeton University Press

Published by Princeton University Press, 41 William Street, Princeton, New Jersey 08540

In the United Kingdom: Princeton University Press, 3 Market Place, Woodstock, Oxfordshire OX20 1SY

Publication of this book has been aided by the French Ministry of Culture-Centre National du Livre

Library of Congress Cataloging-in-Publication Data

Bucaille, Laetitia.
    [Générations intifada. English]
    Growing up Palestinian : Israeli occupation and the Intifada generation / Laetitia Bucaille ; translated by Anthony Roberts.
       p.   cm.—(Princeton studies in Muslim politics)
    Includes index.
    ISBN 0-691-11670-9 (alk. paper)
    1. Intifada, 1987–   2. Israel-Arab War, 1967—Occupied territories.   3. Palestinian Arabs—Politics and government—1993–   I. Title.   II. Series.

    DS119.75.B8313   2004
    956.95'3044—dc22   2003061046

British Library Cataloging-in-Publication Data is available

This book has been composed in Adobe Caslon text with Gill Sans Display

Printed on acid-free paper. ∞

pup.princeton.edu

Printed in the United States of America

10 9 8 7 6 5 4 3 2 1

CONTENTS

FOREWORD

The term "Arab street" enjoyed a brief recent upsurge in popularity. For some, the old connotations of the term still prevail—an undifferentiated and unknowable mass of people with no clear divisions of opinion by class, gender, age, or education, and prone to manipulation. That meaning of the term has been rapidly displaced. Among many policymakers, however, the Arab "street" takes for granted rising educational levels, a greater ease of travel, and the proliferation of new communications media, resulting in greater levels of public accountability.

Ironically, in spite of grueling travel restrictions, a collapsed economy, and schools that often function only intermittently, the opinions of the Palestinians of Gaza and the West Bank have become much better known—and differentiated. One means is through increasingly sophisticated public opinion polling, such as the joint Palestinian-Israeli Public Opinion Poll (www.pcpsr.org) and the public opinion polls of the Jerusalem Media and Communication Centre (www.jmcc.org), conducted regularly since 1993. These polls provide insight into a society with rapidly evolving views on political, social, and economic issues that are often at variance with the received wisdom of the established political elite.

A complementary approach to understanding Palestinian society is what Karl Mannheim called the "social document," the narration of lives or events that, through their fullness, elegance, and clarity, embody a more comprehensive pattern of events and perspectives. The "social document," or ethnographic "thick description," is Laetitia Bucaille's approach in *Growing Up Palestinian*. This book is an updated English translation of *Générations Intifada* (2002) that takes account of events through the spring of 2003. Others have told the story of the first (1987–1994) and second (2000–2002) Palestinian *intifada*s—the Arabic word for "uprising" has become so common in the English-speaking world that it often goes unitalicized—from the top down. Bucaille's view is from the ground level of Palestinian society, from the perspective of Bassam, Sami, Najy, and other *shebab* youth who came of age in resistance against Israeli occupation. For some, a clandestine economy across military frontiers with traffic in contraband, stolen vehicles, alcohol, and drugs became a way of life, while a turn toward increased religiosity provides answers for others. All who came of age during the intifada generations know only cramped social spaces shaped by the daily humiliations of searches, roadblocks, curfews, reprisals, repression, and unemployment. Rarely able to travel beyond their immediate locales, these youth have been daily confronted with the corruption and compromises of life along arbitrary and changing frontiers and occupied societies. These conditions, coupled with for many the hopelessness of ever taking control of their lives, have contributed to nurturing a younger generation that Bucaille describes as "unsullied by pragmatism" yet painfully aware of the need to come to terms with Israeli society.

The outside world experiences life in Palestine and Israel largely through the bleak statistics of the numbers killed on both sides. For life among ordinary Palestinians, *Growing Up Palestinian* offers a gripping narrative, showing the choices and alternatives offered people from many different backgrounds and walks of life, where acts of compromise and expediency are balanced by acts of courage, restraint, and decency in the face of desperate circumstances.

Palestinians debate among themselves whether the suicidal kamikazes in their midst are cynically selected and manipulated by some political leaders, or whether they are the "ultimate expression of Palestinian despair." Bucaille argues that both familiar explanations are overly simplistic. She offers no easy answers, but her account of people coming of age in the context of social and political despair and hopelessness is not unremittingly bleak, nor does it rationalize extremist choices. Many Palestinians, she writes, doubt the effectiveness of armed struggle yet are hard pressed to envisage alternatives. Instead, they see the hope for genuine change as emanating from Israeli society itself, as Israelis recognize the limits of sustained repression.

The consequences of internal debates among Israelis themselves, the growing numbers of non-Jews who have Israeli citizenship, and the growing Israeli awareness that it is in their interest to find ways to come to terms with a viable Palestinian state coexisting with Israel, such reconciliation will not be easy to achieve, but the alternative—the prolonged continuation of present policies—is even harder to contemplate.

Bucaille offers a compelling and vivid account of growing up in the intifada generations. Some turn to hatred, violence, and radicalization, but, seemingly against all odds, others sustain hope and work toward a better social and political world. Through narrating politics and everyday life at "ground zero" as experienced by youth in Palestinian society today, *Growing Up Palestinian* makes an invaluable contribution to understanding the choices and constraints facing both Palestinians and Israelis as they seek alternatives to the cycles of repression, reprisal, and retaliation.

Dale F. Eickelman

James Piscatori

ACKNOWLEDGMENTS

I wish to express my special thanks—and my affection—to Daad, Ghassan, Majad, Umm al-Abid, and Walid, who so freely offered me their friendship, time, and trust. May their lives be long and happy.

I wish to thank the Jaffa Cultural Center for opening its doors to me.

I would also like to express my gratitude to Pierre Aussedat for his syntactical revelations (and to wish a warm welcome to Alfred), to Heikel Ben Sedrine for his unfailing love, to Laurent Carpentier for his dexterity and his freezer, to Faraj Ghunaim for his help and loyalty, to Bibiane de la Roque for her concern and commitment, to Philippe le Roux for testing my resilience, to Jean-Claude Lescure for his rivalry, to Sandrine Rui for her enthusiasm and sharp obeservation, and to Agnès Villechaise-Dupont for her steady advice and encouragement.

My work has received the support and backing of the Laboratoire d'analyse des problèmes sociaux et de l'action collective (LAPSAC) of the University of Bordeaux-II. My thanks are due to its director, Professor Georges Felouzis.

Finally, I thank Marc for his smile and his voice, and Michel for the time he could have claimed for himself, and the wishes he allowed to go unfulfilled.

GLOSSARY

Arabic Terms

al-Asqa Intifada	second Palestinian uprising, which began in September 2000
al-Jazeera	an Arabic-language satellite television network
al-Khtiar	"Old man": the familiar, affectionate nickname given to Yasser Arafat
al-Quds	Arabic name for Jerusalem
Aid	feast marking the end of Ramadan
arak	aniseed-based liquor
dabka	a traditional Palestinian dance for both sexes
falafel	chick-pea fritters, a popular dish in the Middle East
Fatah	largest division of the PLO, founded by Yasser Arafat in the late 1950s
Fathahoui	a member of Fatah
fedayeen	fighters
foul	cooked broad beans
Hamas	The name is based on the Arabic acronym for Islamic Resistance Movement. Hamas began as an offshoot of the Muslim Brothers (an Egyptian paramilitary movement) and is known for its violent methods.
imam	an Islamic religious leader
jawal	a cell phone that works on the system installed by the Palestinian telecommunications company
Jihad	Islamic holy war
keffieh	black-and-white woven Arab scarf
khamsin	a hot wind that blows off the desert, laden with dust in the early spring
kippurs	small, round skullcaps worn by most Jewish men during religious holidays

moukhtar	a system that goes back to Ottoman times, when local representatives presented their group's complaints to the central power. The moukhtar is a traditional headman, and even today he may intervene to settle differences between individuals or families.
nakba	catastrophe (applied to the 1948 creation of Israel and the exile of 854,000 Palestinians)
rais	leader
Shabiba	youth; also the name by which the Youth Committee for Social Action is known
shebab	young man; sheb in the singular. In the Palestinian context, shebab refers to young militants who took part in the Intifada. This criterion of political participation tends to outweigh the age dimension.
zakat	alms. Islam requires the faithful to give a fraction of their income to charity.

Other Terms

DFLP	(Democratic Front for the Liberation of Palestine) a division of the PLO
Ha'aretz	the left-wing Israeli daily newspaper
IDF	(Israeli Defense Forces) the Israeli army
NUC	(National Unified Command) a political organization created during the 1980s as a part of the first Intifada, composed of the four factions that make up the PLO—Fatah, PFLP, DFLP, and PCP.
Old Man (*Al-Khtiar*)	affectionate nickname given to Yassar Arafat
Palestinian Authority	the Palestinian government
PFLP	(Popular Front for the Liberation of Palestine) a left-wing division of the PLO
PCP	(Palestinian Communist Party) a division of the PLO
PLO	(Palestinian Liberation Organization) founded in Cairo in 1964
refuzeniks	Israeli reservists who refuse to serve in the Occupied Territories
shekel	Israeli currency unit
Tsahal	another name for the Israeli Army, from the Hebrew version of the acronym
UNRWA	(United Nations Relief Work Agency) a refugee relief agency within the United Nations

INTRODUCTION

Ariel Sharon's appearance on the Temple Mount in Jerusalem on September 20, 2000, provoked a general conflagration in the Palestinian
Territories. But the real causes of the uprising lie much deeper. Growing frustration with a peace process that had failed to fulfill its promise;
the Palestinians' sense that they had been cheated by the Israelis, their
negotiating partners, who felt similarly cheated; the absence of a political perspective made palpable by the failure of the July 2000 Camp
David summit; and a general dissatisfaction with the administration of
the Palestinian Authority all explain the eagerness of young people and
militants on the West Bank and Gaza to take up the cudgels of Palestinian nationalism yet again, in a direct confrontation with Israel. Called
the al-Aqsa Intifada by the Israeli media, this second uprising in the
occupied Palestinian territories since 1967 bears little resemblance to the
1987 Intifada, which was organized along the lines of civil resistance.
Nevertheless, both Palestinians and Israelis call it by the same name.

What is this revolt about?

The real question concerns the political direction of the al-Aqsa
Intifada. Are we looking at one more convulsion in a conflict between
two irreconcilable peoples that has been going on for a century past? Or
should we see recent events as a stage in the Palestinian nation's struggle for liberation, perhaps the final stretch of the road to an independent
state? The absence of any political perspective on the issue would seem
to favor the first hypothesis; yet the vigor of the Palestinian demands

and the powerlessness of the Israelis to prolong their occupation forever point to the second.

Given the failure of the political negotiating process, the Palestinians are relying on physical defiance in their struggle for self-determination. Yet two brands of logic—one Palestinian, the other Israeli—may impede progress toward this outcome, and even prevent it altogether.

In the first place, there is no doubt that the weaknesses and contradictions of the militant Palestinian movement have dimmed the prospects for national liberation. The participants in the latest uprising are poorly organized, their goals and their methods are often at odds, and many of them tend to be isolated from the general run of Palestinian society. The al-Aqsa Intifada is not a structured movement that encompasses the entire Palestinian population. Furthermore, the Palestinian Authority, obliged as it is to represent Palestinians in international negotiations, is in a false position vis-à-vis the armed combatants it needs to control.

There have been several distinct phases and types of action. In its early months, the uprising basically consisted of demonstrations in the course of which teenagers hurled rocks at heavily equipped soldiers and tanks. The killing of children and young Palestinians that followed seemed pointless and futile, and it shocked international public opinion; in particular, the shooting by the Israeli Army of a terrified little boy, Mohammed al-Dura, who had run to his father for protection and died in his arms, provoked outrage all over the world. The images of the child's death demonstrated the hopeless inequality of the two sides, and the disproportionate use of military force by Israel. But the Palestinian gains in the media were short-lived and were quickly reversed by other scenes of extreme violence, such as the savage lynching of four Israelis by an angry Ramallah mob. Moreover, the impact of such images on the way the Palestinian question was perceived in the wider world was relatively limited, their principal effect being to reinforce the convictions of a public that had already made up its mind one way or another. For some, the exaggerated numbers of Palestinian children and teenagers killed by Israeli bullets was a sign of the cowardice of their parents, who permitted and even encouraged their young to confront the Israeli Defense Force (IDF). For others, they demonstrated for the umpteenth time the cruelty and inadequacy of what the Israelis were doing. To rely on a strategy of winning over international public opinion, using the media as a vehicle, was an uncertain and perilous course of action. On a national level, the pointless slaughter of the stone-throwers froze Palestinian society into the posture of victim, demonstrating its utter inability to come up with any more effective means of resisting the occupying power.

More recently, beginning in April 2001, armed groups mostly affiliated with Fatah adopted the tactic of attacking Israeli settlements and army posts in the West Bank and Gaza. Despite a few daring and successful coups, this resort to arms had little effect given that the young Palestinian fighters, acting intermittently, were not conducting anything like a coordinated guerrilla war, and the repression of activists that followed their raids further weakened the broader Palestinian movement of armed struggle. The cordoning off of the Palestinian Territories, the closing of roads between Palestinian localities, the repeated occupation of certain zones that had previously been autonomous, and the destruction by bulldozers or by missiles fired by F16 fighter-bombers at houses and civil and military buildings were too high a price to pay. In consequence, Palestinian solidarity with this brand of armed struggle has grown more and more tenuous.

The political class, the intellectuals, and a good proportion of the middle classes basically see this mode of combat as wrong-headed. In their view, the Palestinians have nothing to gain from a military confrontation. Instead they advocate the organization of civil resistance to the Israeli occupation. Nevertheless, the vigor of the methods used by the IDF and the absence of any direct communication with the structures of the Israeli government that were replaced by the Palestinian Authority are considerable handicaps to such resistance.

The armed elements within the two Islamist groups have now gone back to the practice of suicide bombings against Israeli civilians. Since the beginning of the Intifada there has been a steady succession of deadly attacks. Unlike other modes of action, suicide bombings provide the Palestinians with a means of inflicting significant losses on Israel, thereby momentarily tipping the balance in their favor. Lately, Fatah activists have begun imitating Islamist methods. But these particularly murderous tactics have had the effect of radicalizing Israeli society, shoring up the Israeli administration's security policy and steadily stripping away Palestinian legitimacy on the international scene. Meanwhile the brutal repression carried out by the Israeli state has the reverse effect of recruiting ever more Palestinian extremists to the cause.

The present impasse stems from the fact that Israel has now opted for a military strategy, where it has an unassailable advantage. The government of Ehud Barak, while it was pursuing its negotiations with representatives of the Palestinian Authority, engaged in a cycle of vigorous repression. Ariel Sharon, who was elected in February 2001, intensified the policy of tit-for-tat reprisals and broke off talks with Yasser Arafat, whom he held ultimately responsible for the suicide attacks. In demanding a halt to the Intifada as a precondition for a resumption of the peace process, the new Israeli prime minister again showed that he viewed Palestinian violence as a simple question of maintaining public order. He refused point blank to consider the situation in the light of a political impasse. Furthermore, Ariel Sharon was able to take skillful advantage of the new international context that followed the events of September 11, 2001. His argument consisted of placing those responsible for the attack on the World Trade Center on the same footing as those who were carrying out suicide missions against Israeli civilians. He publicly concluded that the head of the Palestinian Authority was not only responsible for the violence but also quite incapable of providing effective government in the Territories. This double charge of guilt and impotence may have been a contradiction in terms, but Ariel Sharon's comparison of Yasser Arafat with Osama Bin Laden was more or less acknowledged by leaders in United States and met only a mild protest from the European Union. Israeli public opinion showed itself overwhelmingly favorable to the notion that the president of the Palestinian Authority should be put out of action, reverting to the attitude that prevailed in the early 1990s, whereby the head of the Palestine Liberation Organization (PLO) was seen as the "leader of a terrorist organization." Disappointed and confused by the Palestinians' rejection of the Camp David peace terms in July 2000, which at the time had seemed to most Israelis not only unprecedented but also very generous, a sizable section of the Israeli left fell into line behind the rightist government. Each of the protagonists has regressed in the estimation of the other, leaving less and less leeway for political action.

It is clear that the absence of a political solution continues to cost the Palestinians very dearly. It is also clear that, in the end, Israel will be made to pay for it in equal measure. The most immediate cost is in human lives. The Israeli Army's security measures and the means at its disposal cannot entirely protect the nation against determined suicide bombers. In the longer term, if Israel does not resign itself to complete separation from the Palestinians and to the creation of a state within the territories delineated in 1967, it will have to reckon with a large and unruly Arab population within its own borders. Indeed, it will have to bestow citizenship on this sizable minority, if it is not to renounce its own democratic principles. The catch is that if it does so, it will also have to renounce the Jewish character of the Israeli state, and for this reason most Israelis reject the idea out of hand.

Are Palestinians and Israelis fated never to bridge the gulf that stands between them, and find peace?

This book is intended as a record of the experience of certain individual Palestinians on the West Bank and in the Gaza Strip. In exploring the political and personal odysseys of these people, the main objective is to explain the tilt away from the peace process toward the implacable logic of war. The will for a return to the strategy of confrontation, which inhabits so many Palestinians, does not necessarily imply a total rejection of coexistence with the Jewish state. Many of the young people who are trying to organize a guerrilla war and who experienced combat against Israel at the time of the first Intifada are in reality quite pragmatic and open to a whole range of compromises. The attainment of Palestinian autonomy in 1994 raised high hopes among the population, before it became obvious that this political solution was actually designed to perpetuate firm Israeli control over the Territories, and that true sovereignty had eluded the Palestinians. Their disappointment and bitterness were compounded by promises made at the time of the accords and subsequently broken, and by the realization that their own leaders were incapable of achieving the goal of national liberation. The al-Aqsa Intifada is a consequence of this disappointment, and also of the ongoing development of political relationships within the Palestinian community. For in the end, the history of the Palestinian confrontation with Israel is inseparable from the history of the Palestinians' confrontation with themselves.

Growing Up Palestinian

CHAPTER ONE

The Palestinian Intifada: The Revolt against Israeli Occupation, 1987–1994

April 2001: an evening in Nablus. The air was heavy because the *khamsin* was still blowing. Waves of heat flowed across the town, boxed in by the surrounding hills. Suddenly, a crackle of gunfire. A group of *shebab* was attacking an Israeli Army post on one of the hilltops above Nablus. Over the last six months, the army had reoccupied certain strategic points, which allowed it to protect Israeli settlements or to defend against potential attack from the Palestinians.

That day, a few young men had gone up the hill with M16s slung on their backs and portable phones at their belts. They were prepared to take risks. They approached the Israeli soldiers in a stealthy attempt to take them by surprise. But they were spotted by the soldiers, who returned fire, protected by their bullet-proof vests and the walls they had built around their position. The shebab did not immediately retreat. The soldiers quickly outflanked them, and the group was beginning to wonder if this might turn out to be their final sortie, when Sami's cell phone (*jawal*) rang. The caller was Sami's girlfriend, Iman, who had heard the gunfire from where she was, in her family's house down in the Balata refugee camp. Sami was far from reassuring. "This is goodbye," he said. Iman was speechless.

Two hours passed. Iman, down in the camp, was torn between her desperation for news and her fear of endangering Sami's life by distracting his attention. Meanwhile Sami and his friends searched for a way out of the trap that was steadily closing on them. They called the mayor of Nablus on his cell phone to demand that he switch off the street lighting immediately in the zone where they were stranded. After a few hours, the shebab managed to slip back to the Balata camp in the darkness.

Later Sami and three others were sitting in his bedroom, drinking coffee and steadily filling an ashtray with butt-ends. Najy and Bassam were Sami's childhood friends, companions in battle, detention, and exile; the third youth, Fuad, was also from the camp.* When the wave of anger engulfed the Territories in the fall of 2000, they set up their group as a presence to be reckoned with on the ground. The earliest confrontations with the Israelis took place around the tomb of Joseph in Nablus, which was kept under guard by soldiers because a few Jews came there regularly to pray. This place was a flashpoint during the confrontations of September 1996, which were set off by the opening of an archaeologist's tunnel adjoining the al-Aqsa Mosque in Jerusalem. Several Israeli soldiers lost their lives there. In October 2000 the tomb of the prophet again became a flashpoint for conflict, when Israeli soldiers as well as Palestinian civilians and police were killed there. The Israeli losses were sufficiently high to induce the IDF to negotiate a retreat, abandoning the holy place to the protection of Palestinian forces. After the evacuation of the tomb, tensions fell for a while. The cycle of confrontation began again in March 2001, at which time several teenagers were shot by the Israeli army in the course of demonstrations on the road from al-Quds (Arabic name for Jerusalem), leading to an Israeli Army roadblock. In reprisal, armed groups of Palestinians began firing on Israeli positions.

Sami, Najy, Bassam, and Fuad made their attacks less frequently, while keeping themselves supplied with weapons and staying on the alert. They knew they were wanted by the Israeli Army, and because of this they kept constantly on the move, within an area of several square kilometers. By day, they avoided the high ground around Nablus where they might be arrested at army checkpoints or recognized by soldiers watching from the hilltops. Sami spent part of the day asleep, and a lot

---

*Sami, Najy, and Bassam are the main protagonists in this book: like everyone else mentioned here, they are real people, but pseudonyms are used throughout this book. Their life stories are recounted in chapters 1, 2, and 5.

of time talking to Iman on his cell phone. His friends assembled in his room, where he lived with his bed, a television, a computer, armchairs, a coffee table, and a few pieces of furniture containing his clothes and possessions.

Sami and Najy have been inseparable since childhood. Their families are both large and impecunious, neighbors in the camp; the two boys went to school together. At first sight Sami seems calm and poised, serious and brooding. This first impression soon fades when he unleashes his savage sense of humor. He is never without his windbreaker, as if he's planning to jump up and leave at any moment.

Najy would be handsome, if it weren't for his deeply lined face and air of lurking aggression. His manner is brusque; he's impulsive when he speaks and quick to pull his gun. Meeting him with Bassam for the first time, you would take them for brothers. They are the same medium height, and their thin bodies bear the marks of their present clandestine existence and of the hunger strikes they endured in jail. Bassam is the oldest in the group. He has a mature, responsible side that makes him more accessible than the others.

When Najy was seven, he sewed together a Palestinian flag and went with Sami to join a Palestinian demonstration that was marching by the camp. That evening his parents thrashed him. A year later his father died, leaving Najy's mother with eight sons and three daughters to take care of.

Najy was always a handful. When they were thirteen, he and Sami physically threatened a teacher who had expelled one of them from school for a few days. Shortly after, they and some other boys cobbled together a home-made gun and let it off in the general direction of an Israeli settlement. Sami got off scot-free and nobody denounced him. But in 1985 Najy, who wasn't yet fourteen, was arrested and sentenced to five years in prison by an Israeli military court. He remembers how he burst into tears when he heard the verdict. Then he became overwhelmed with fury. "When the judge handed down the sentence, I punched my lawyer [who is Palestinian] and I spat on the judge. I said: 'You're sending a kid to prison, but you'll see, a man will walk out again!'"

What sort of man? If the goal of the Israeli military administration was to neutralize adolescents like Najy, it failed spectacularly. Behind bars, the men of Najy's generation were hardened, and in addition they received a solid political education. Intrepid, rebellious youths were turned into highly politicized militants, fully integrated into a structured organization. The Israeli prisons provided a veritable school for thousands of young men like Najy. Taken in hand by their elders, who had created the first resistance networks affiliated with the PLO and who were serving long stretches as a result, the younger generation found themselves beginning or completing an ideological and militant apprenticeship.

In prison Najy found himself with Bassam, who raised his spirits. Bassam had already served several months of his first sentence. At fifteen, he had been a member of Fatah for two years, one of a group that had tried to attack Israeli patrols with Molotov cocktails. Najy, who also identified with Fatah, officially signed up with the organization in prison.[1] Sami, meanwhile, did not share his friends' fate until two years later, when he also went to prison.

Fatah, a political party founded in the 1950s by members of the Palestinian diaspora, originally became popular in the Territories when its fedayeen distinguished themselves in guerrilla warfare against Israel in the 1970s. At that time, Fatah's leaders, first in Jordan and later in Lebanon, did not count on Palestinians in Gaza and the West Bank to open a front to resist Israel. But during that decade contacts were made and the first networks were built up in both locations. After the PLO's defeat in Lebanon and its exile in Tunisia, Palestinian militants within the Territories concluded that political structures and engagements had to be created within Palestinian society as a whole. The Israeli military occupiers banned Fatah, and the army relentlessly hunted down its people. They responded in 1981 by founding an association, the Youth Committee for Social Action, better known as the Shabiba. Officially, its objective was nonpolitical, but in fact the Shabiba was a vehicle for recruiting militants and for providing Fatah with a legal front.

Groups proliferated in the secondary schools, universities, and certain city quarters. At first they focused on cultural activities and mutual assistance. Through this association, Fatah rapidly increased its membership, catching up with the leftist groups that had been operating in the Territories since the 1970s. The movement could call on considerable financial resources, and its message was both accessible and attractive: as a self-proclaimed revolutionary group, it refused to lock itself into any given ideological dialectic. Its broad, stated purpose was to unite the Palestinian people, whatever their individual beliefs and political convictions.

As a result, by the 1980s Fatah had become the most popular political movement in the Territories. All its energies now had to be concentrated on the liberation of Palestine, which, as the PLO's founding charter made crystal clear, was incompatible with the existence of Israel. Ideology was put aside, and priority was given to ways and means of waging the war for independence.

INSIDE ISRAEL'S PRISONS

Bassam likes to make comparisons between the prisons he has known. His first was in Hebron, where he endured a series of interrogations. "To begin with, it was really tough. Fifteen is very young to go through that. The winter in Hebron was freezing and our cells were bitterly cold. It was snowing outside, but in spite of it there were cockroaches everywhere. The interrogations stretched me to the limit, physically and psychologically. Some guys had serious after effects; a few lost their minds completely."

After that Bassam was transferred to the Nablus jail, where he was warmly welcomed by the other prisoners and included in a program of activities that local Fatah leaders had developed. As a revolutionary organization, Fatah expected steady discipline and sustained moral effort. The forty inmates in each cell woke at 7 every morning. After a cursory wash, the prisoners were counted by the administrators. After this, the duties and obligations established by the Palestinians themselves came into play. The prisoners were expected to study subjects of their own choice for several hours. Later, an extended period was allowed for group discussion of political topics, the purpose being to instruct the younger inmates in the history of Palestine and to sow the seeds of a political education. Sports were also practiced, and prisoners were allowed two hours a day to themselves. From morning to night, their time was precisely regulated.

Hussam Khader, ten years older than Bassam, was one of the initiators of this program in the Nablus prison.[2] A Fatah official in the Balata camp, Khader had an appetite for organization and responsibility. For him the struggle against the occupation required quasi-military discipline and a thorough purging of personal habits. Najy says he found his own rebellious spirit at odds with Hussam's plans on an almost daily basis. For example, the older man and his friends were set on banning the use of strong tobacco by the young prisoners. This provoked such a backlash that rationing cigarettes had to be adopted as a compromise. Hussam Khader, a man of principle, could be harsh, but in the end he won the respect of shebab like Bassam and Najy. Khader too had been sent to prison very young. He was first arrested in 1979, at the age of seventeen: "I was in jail for eighteen days and I met prisoners who talked about Fatah and the revolution," he recalls. "That's when I started taking an active interest in politics."

After a couple of years in the Nablus jail, Bassam was sent back to Hebron. The Israeli administration had not changed its attitude, indeed its violence had considerably intensified. "Two or three times a month, the soldiers tossed tear gas canisters into the cells. Or else there was a collective punishment and we had to stand stark naked in the yard while they beat us with sticks and iron rods. Most of the soldiers came from the settlements and were ultrareligious; they were the ones who really loathed us. They were totally different from the more liberal type of Israeli. In the Nablus jail, a prisoners' representative could go and see the governor and present him with requests. At least he listened, even though most of the time he said no. And every time he said no, we went on a hunger strike," explains Bassam.

Family visits were authorized once every two weeks, for half an hour. Prisoners' relatives stood waiting patiently outside the gates, in all weather. At the Hebron detention center they were often mistreated by the Israeli guards, even though it was a longish trip from Nablus, which is at the northern end of the West Bank. The visitors first had to take a collective taxi to Ramallah, fifty kilometers away, then another from Ramallah to Bethlehem. If they had no valid pass to cross Jerusalem, they had to skirt the Holy City and take a route three times longer. Even when they reached Bethlehem, it was still another twenty kilometers to Hebron.

Bassam's mother was the one who visited him most often. Every Friday she went to see one of her three sons, each of whom was in a different jail.

After Hebron, Bassam was transferred yet again. His last two years of incarceration were spent in the prison of Jneid, near Nablus, a special detention center for men serving long sentences. Here too the penitentiary regime was ferocious. But Bassam derived a certain comfort from being with prisoners who were older than he was, more experienced and more hardened. During this period, he read a great deal. He learned Hebrew along with a little English. The sessions were cut short when the cellmate who was teaching him the language of Shakespeare was moved to another prison before he could impart all he knew.

In this way many a Palestinian schoolboy and student serving a sentence managed to acquire some form of knowledge in prison. Foreign languages, notably Hebrew, were popular. Mastery of the occupier's tongue was necessary for anyone who wanted a diploma, and the prison administration authorized prisoners to follow the program of the Hebrew University of Jerusalem, the only one available to them. Correspondence courses were given in Hebrew and had to be paid for; prisoners were forbidden to take courses in Arabic given by a Palestinian university. From time to time, a professor came out to answer questions on each subject; exams were organized in the prison. As a rule, the Palestinians who chose the academic option tended to be those serving very long sentences.

Bassam was released on January 16, 1991, the day the international coalition began its attack on Iraq.[3] On that day, and thereafter for the duration of the Gulf War, the Occupied Territories were placed under a blanket curfew while Iraq—intent on spreading the conflict throughout the region—bombarded Israel. For two hours a day, every other day, the Israeli Army lifted its restrictions so Palestinian families could go out and buy food and supplies. For forty consecutive days, the people of the West Bank and the Gaza Strip were unable to work or study—indeed, the majority were unable to earn any money at all. They just sat at home, locked in, fainting with anxiety and boredom; the only relief was an occasional visit to neighbors or a game of cards.

So Bassam came out of prison to find his hometown empty and deserted. He was unable to get his bearings, let alone find his way home. Soldiers detailed to supervise the curfew apprehended him, then let him go. Alone again, he knocked on a stranger's door: he was welcomed and plied with tea, and an ambulance was called to take him out to the Balata refugee camp. His family, neighbors, and friends flocked around, but he soon found out that the freedom he had returned to was limited in the extreme. For over a month, until the end of the Gulf War, Bassam was confined to the darkened interior of his family's house. Palestinian society, sorely tried by these events, became completely turned in on itself.

THE PALESTINIAN UNDERGROUND

In the spring of that year, life returned to a semblance of normality. The pressure exerted by the army was relaxed a little in the towns. Bassam passed his exams and resumed his political activities. This was soon noticed, and in the fall a detachment of Israeli soldiers ransacked his house and demanded that he turn himself in. Bassam's response was to go underground. He stopped sleeping at home and kept moving quietly from one house to another—always within the Balata camp. Najy, suspected of taking part in the killing of a collaborator, was also wanted by the Israeli Army, and at this time Bassam joined forces with Sami and Najy to form a secret armed cell. Seven other young men from Balata volunteered, making contact with the PLO in Amman and Tunis to obtain material support. They maintained links with the local resistance command structures while preserving complete freedom of action. Armed with a few light weapons, they concentrated their attacks on army patrols and Israeli settlers. Most of the time they hid alongside roads, waiting for targets to pass by, then briefly opened fire and ran. A few times they were successful. Bassam says: "Our goal has always been to liberate our country. We're realists and we recognize the principle of the two states living side by side. To win back our rights in our own land, we must use both political and military means. The occupation prevents us from living as we wish to. We need a revolution to force a change."

The shebab agreed with Fatah's stance. They disapproved of attacks on Israeli civilians and restricted their operations to the perimeter of the Occupied Territories. Furthermore they avoided facing the awkward question of collaborators. Informers recruited by the Israeli Army were legion in the Territories, and whether attracted by the prospect of gain, victims of blackmail, or otherwise manipulated, they provided the occupation forces with a constant trickle of intelligence. When the Intifada began, its leaders attempted to neutralize the network of collaborators. Some were kept under surveillance and placed under a kind of de facto house arrest; as a warning, they might be physically attacked, perhaps shot at. The ones that were thought to be irrecoverably dangerous were killed. The job of doing the killing was left to the shebab, and some of them even made it a specialty, leaving the battle against the Israeli Army to others. Executions proliferated, and often the vigilantes did not bother to doublecheck on what might have been no more than baseless suspicions against certain individuals. The campaign reached such a pitch that Yasser Arafat himself finally intervened, calling for a halt to the murders of collaborators in the Territories.

Bassam's group tried to distance itself from the vigilante role. All the same, on two separate occasions Najy was compelled to take action. "I shot one collaborator near the Nablus town hall. He was a well-known intelligence agent, and he openly consorted with the army. I went up to him and asked if his name was such and such. He said yes, and I shot him dead. You mustn't think it's an easy thing, to kill somebody. I was shaking like a leaf and I had nightmares all the following night. But the second time wasn't so bad. The target was a Palestinian policeman who went on working for the Israeli government even though he'd been told to resign several times. He was at the wheel of his car. I climbed in beside him. I verified his identity in the same way; he realized what was up and there was a struggle. That really annoyed me and I let him have it—six bullets in the body. Sami came and got me out of there and we ran like hell, because the Israelis were starting to show up."

It wasn't so much the regular army patrols that worried the shebab, it was the Israeli special forces. With a view to raising the effectiveness of the repression and destroying all Palestinian military and political networks, the IDF adopted new tactics. Special units were formed, made up of Israelis who were identical in looks and speech to the Palestinians themselves. They even took "integration courses" in Arab villages. To avoid suspicion and look as harmless as possible, they disguised themselves as women or old men. A parcel swaddled like a baby, a veil, a false beard, a cane, a *keffieh* knotted in the fashion favored by masked shebab who wanted to stay anonymous—these were some of the ruses of the Israeli military elite. They invariably knew everything about the Palestinians they targeted, and when they struck it was with lightning speed. They would suddenly materialize, shoot their victim, and melt away as quickly as they had come.

In 1992 Bassam's group found itself caught in the toils of Israeli military intelligence. The army arrested five of their number. Twice in the space of a few weeks, special forces swept into the Balata camp. The first attack left dead three young men who had been scheduled to meet Bassam, Sami, and Najy a few minutes later. The second time, Bassam himself had a close call: he was in a narrow alley in the camp, talking to Khaled, one of his group, and Yussef, a Fatah member who was also wanted by the Israelis. For some trivial reason, Bassam had to drop by his home for a couple of minutes. On his way back to the other two, he heard shots and immediately grasped what was happening. He yelled at the boys in the street to pelt the special forces unit with stones and cause a diversion. Khaled was mortally wounded, but Yussef managed to get away—though he was picked up a few weeks later and sentenced to twenty-five years in jail. Again, Bassam had missed death by a whisker. The Israelis grabbed Khaled's body and melted away.

Because of the boldness of these attacks, the Balata camp was no longer a secure base for the group's operations. The shebab had to resort to more radical measures; it was no longer enough simply to avoid sleeping at home. The army now came by at regular intervals and pressured families to make their militants give themselves up. Objects and furniture were smashed, and brothers and nephews arrested. The shebab spent more and more time concealed in the hills, sometimes in holes underground. Hidden like this, they kept themselves fed as well as they could, chain-smoked cigarettes, watched, and waited for the information and supplies brought to them by their contacts. They shivered in freezing temperatures, rain, and snow as they moved deeper into the countryside. All the time they struggled to maintain contact with other armed groups in Nablus and the West Bank. Only occasionally did they risk a sortie to the camp or the town. The shebab could count on the support of the families that lodged them, fed them, and kept them informed of the army's movements; nevertheless, life was precarious in the extreme. Despite the tip-offs they received and the elaborate precautions they took, despite their weapons and their practiced guile,

Bassam, Sami, and Najy were living on borrowed time, and they knew it. The IDF's intelligence services had never given up trying to capture or kill them—far from it.

In July 1992 the three went to al-Najah University, in the hills of Nablus. They had a rendezvous there with one of their contacts. The meeting was not expected to last very long, but even so there was time for the Israeli Army to swoop down and seal the entire campus. The three wanted shebab were alerted, but too late. Nevertheless, they had no intention of giving themselves up, and consequently the army laid siege to the university. Not a single student, teacher, or administrative employee was allowed to go in or out of the campus zone. Life went on—more or less—in the classrooms, in the cafeteria, and on the grounds, except that the five thousand students were not allowed to leave.

There was overwhelming support for the three shebab among the students. They insisted that the outlaws in their midst should stand up to the Israeli Army, even if they themselves suffered for it. The armed shebab were greatly admired, seen as heroes ready to sacrifice themselves for a political ideal. Their courage and coolness were remarkable under the circumstances, and the mystique surrounding their actions raised their status among the students to great heights. Bassam, Sami, and Najy were deeply moved when people offered to surrender in their stead. After seventy-two hours, the cafeteria ran out of water and provisions and some of the students were taken ill. Outside, negotiations were under way among the Israeli military, the International Red Cross, and the Palestinian political representative. The IDF began by demanding that thirty-nine people be turned over to them, but this was flatly refused. The number was finally negotiated down to six. This compromise averted prison for the activists but did not exactly let them go free: they were banished from Israel on the spot. A vehicle supplied by the Red Cross transported them over the border to Jordan. The siege had lasted four days.

FORCED EXILE

Throughout their journey to the border, the shebab had the impression that the army was on their heels. They were afraid they would be shot. But in the end they crossed the Jordan unscathed and drove on to Amman, where they were met by the Palestinian ambassador and some Fatah officials from the West Bank who had been thrown out by the Israelis four years earlier. Marwan Barghuti, the Fatah leader in Ramallah, and Tayssir Nasrallah from the Balata refugee camp, who was president of the Shabiba committee in Nablus, were among them; they were now employed in the PLO's western department.[4]

Bassam spent his first two months in Jordan being interrogated every morning by Jordanian intelligence. "It was incredible! Here were these Jordanians, who were supposed to be our allies and supporters, squeezing me as hard as they could for information about Fatah. For two months they never left me alone. When I realized what was going on, it was a heavy blow. Today they won't let me back into Jordan."

As soon as they had their Jordanian passports,[5] in late 1992, the three friends moved on to Iraq, where they lived for two years and concentrated on their studies. Bassam opted for a management diploma, while Sami and Najy studied for, and received, their bachelor's degrees. Every three months they went back to Amman to pick up the funds the PLO had allotted for their upkeep.

Despite the effect of the Gulf War on Iraqi society and the Iraqi economy, the shebab of Balata were happy in Baghdad. Bassam says it was the happiest time of his life. "I felt free. I could go wherever I liked. It was nothing like Jordan. Even though it wasn't much of a democracy if you were an Iraqi, and even though there were real economic problems as a result of the embargo, as a Palestinian I felt completely free—free to move around, to say what I chose. And at last I saw something of the world outside. I made plenty of friends. The Iraqis appreciated us."

Najy too reveled in his newfound freedom. He'd heard there were prostitutes in Baghdad, but at first he didn't know where to find them. In the restaurant of a hotel, a woman accompanied by children beckoned him across to her table. Najy suspected nothing at the time—it was only later that one of the hotel employees tipped him off that the woman was turning tricks. Najy came across her a second time; he was intrigued and decided to ask her why she was doing what she did. The reply was, to pay for her youngest daughter's eye operation. Shocked, Najy immediately offered to pay for the whole lot. The mother became his first lover.

During his stay in Iraq, he also tried alcohol for the first time and discovered its effects. In the house where he and his friends lived, there was no objection to girls and drinking. Bassam, who prayed every day of his life, tended to distance himself from all this. Not so Najy: as time went on his sexual experiences multiplied, along with his mistresses. He remembers how he found out that one of them was the wife of a colonel in the Iraqi intelligence service, and how he panicked and abruptly cut off all relations when he found out. Then he fell in love with a woman whose husband was frequently traveling away from home. Najy spent night after sleepless night in her bed. Her name was Hanan, and he named his eldest daughter after her.

On one of their trips to Amman, the three friends were introduced to Yasser Arafat as the heroes of Nablus. Najy couldn't believe it. He kept saying to Marwan Barghuti beside him: "Did I really just meet Abu Ammar?" All he can remember is that Arafat was tiny, and his hand as he shook it was tiny, too.

As time went by, the Palestinian exiles saw more and more of each other and forged close friendships. Najy became Barghuti's protégé; Tayssir Nasrallah and his wife took good care of the three shebab, and together they contrived to re-create some of the atmosphere of Balata.

They were paying the price of the Israeli policy of banishing Palestinian activists, which began in the 1970s and was steadily stepped up throughout the 1980s. Considering that men like Barghuti and Nasrallah bore a heavy responsibility for political agitation in the Territories, the Hebrew state hoped to smother the rebellion by simply removing them from the scene. But this policy failed to stop either the planning or the perpetuation of the Intifada. Operating out of Amman, Baghdad, or Tunis, by hook or by crook the first generation of Fatah activists managed to stay in touch with their successors in the field.

THE MANAGEMENT OF THE INTIFADA

After serving his sentence in Nablus, Hussam Khader was forced to leave the Occupied Territories in early 1988, before the outbreak of the Intifada. Tayssir Nasrallah was obliged to follow a year later. Both men had a long history of militant action. Born in the early 1960s in the Balata refugee camp, they had worked together as Fatah operatives setting up a political structure in the place where they lived. They recruited from the Shabiba and formed networks that covered the entire camp. The various quarters were defined and named after the towns or villages from which the refugees had come. Each was placed under the responsibility of its own team of militants. The committees organized camp sanitation, helped the poorer families, and planned anti-Israeli demonstrations.

The struggle against the Israeli occupation also required that Balata should be purged of people whom the militants felt to be negative and harmful, such as consumers of hashish and alcohol, Israeli informers, and common delinquents. All these were ordered to change their ways and bow to the code of morality imposed by the militants. The latter belonged to a new generation that had known little else but the Israeli occupation; driven by a deep sense of outrage, this generation was now gradually mobilizing, and its political idealism led it to embrace principles of outright revolution. Society had to transform itself, to work on itself until it was strong enough to confront the Israeli enemy head on. The militants were both rigorous in their organizational methods and relentlessly single-minded. They caught up many young people in their slipstream. In the Balata refugee camp, their isolated clashes with the Israelis turned out to be a prelude to the general outbreak of the Intifada.

The *Fathahoui* (Arab term for Fatah member) of the camp are adamant that in fact the Intifada began with them, in 1982, at Balata. According to them, the people of the camp were made to pay dearly for their struggle against the occupants. Under the aegis of the Shabiba, Balata initiated its own form of rebellion. "Stones were thrown day and night in Balata, even though there were army lookouts on the rooftops for weeks on end. Molotov cocktails became such a problem that the

IDF patrols avoided the center of the camp as much as they could."[6] The refugee camps, traditionally the main flashpoints of rebellion in the Occupied Territories, indeed provided the earliest symptoms of a more general uprising. In this sense, the Intifada demonstrated that a new group of young men from the ordinary working classes had broken into the political arena.

On December 9, 1987, an IDF jeep crashed into a vehicle carrying Palestinian workers employed in Israel, four of whom were killed. A rumor quickly spread that the accident had been deliberately set up to murder Palestinians. Within hours, a wave of spontaneous fury had engulfed the Jabalya camp at the northern end of the Gaza Strip, and Israeli Army observation posts were attacked by hundreds of angry demonstrators. The revolt spread through the other camps, the working class areas and the towns of Gaza and the West Bank.

The political cells quickly understood the broad nature of this movement and resolved to take control of it using the structures already in place. They plunged into the breach and transformed what had begun as a spontaneous rising into a prolonged revolt. A National Unified Command (NUC) was created, bringing together the four factions that made up the PLO, namely, Fatah, the Popular Front for the Liberation of Palestine (PFLP), the Democratic Front for the Liberation of Palestine (DFLP), and the Palestinian Communist Party (PCP). The goal was to ally the different political forces with a view to assembling the widest possible spectrum of Palestinian society. Representatives of the different formations, now members of the NUC, worked out a program for the rebellion. On a basis of compromise, they regularly set out their strategic aims and circulated written communiqués containing precise directives. Thus the people's committees that had formed spontaneously in each quarter came under the control of the politicians. They now not only relayed the orders put out by the NUC but also took responsibility for carrying them out. Within a very short time they were outlawed by the Israeli military administration and forced underground.

The Islamist organizations, however, refused to subscribe to the NUC, preferring to stay independent. Yet they remained fully active, producing their own tracts, forming action groups, and maintaining leadership contacts with the NUC to coordinate their efforts.

Thus the political movements were directly responsible neither for the outbreak of the Intifada, nor for the demonstrations, nor for the forming of people's committees in December 1987. Instead they reaped the harvest from years of careful groundwork. The militants trained by the Shabiba, the Muslim Brothers, or the Marxist left in the 1970s and 1980s were now operational, and it was they who filled the ranks and command structures of the Intifada.

The NUC now developed a plan of action aimed at disconnecting Palestinian society from the structures of the occupying power. Its tracts advocated a boycott of Israeli administrative acts and products, nonpayment of value-added tax by shopkeepers and traders, and the resignation of functionaries employed by the Israeli civil service, notably the police. Moreover, a communiqué exhorted Palestinian workers to stop selling their labor within Israel. Impelled by its political militants, the general population threw its support behind the civil disobedience movement, and the Intifada's first year ended with the population still overwhelmingly favorable to it.

On several occasions, the leaders of the movement re-evaluated the objectives they had set, in light of the population's capacity to adapt. The call to quarantine Israeli employers was abandoned—obviously, because far too many families in the West Bank and Gaza depended on the wage of a father or a brother working in an Israeli restaurant or building site. On the other hand, the injunction against Palestinians in the Israeli police force was upheld; anyone disobeying could expect a visit from the shebab whose job it was to enforce obedience to the NUC's decrees. The timing of strikes and demonstrations was also decided in this way, and the application of orders emanating from the NUC demonstrated such unity among the population that, in order to break it, Israel's military actually forced tradesmen to raise their steel shutters and do business under duress.

Demonstrations consisted of confrontations between the population (mostly young people) and Israeli troops. The former threw stones; the latter responded with tear gas and rubber bullets. This unequal struggle became a daily occurrence. People even got used to it. In the eyes of the wider world, the televised images of street combat in occupied Palestine came to symbolize the resistance of the entire Palestinian people to the power of Israel. The Intifada was seen as a war in which one side threw stones and the other fired guns. But this was only the visible side of the struggle. Its basic dynamic was very different.

The leaders of the NUC had to find means of satisfying the human needs that had been exposed by the military repression. In the short term, provisions were needed to keep families going during the curfews. More systematically, the planners of the Intifada sought to create the conditions for genuine self-sufficiency by establishing alternative Palestinian networks that were in no way connected to Israel. Their program of action aimed to prove that the Palestinians within the Occupied Territories had sufficient resources to run their own affairs, thus demolishing the argument whereby the integration of the West Bank and the Gaza Strip into Israel was an irreversible and necessary process. This effort of internal organization also demonstrated a determination to transform Palestinian society and its members, to improve their sense of responsibility and collective interest along with their aptitude to resist the occupation and subvert its rules. Every skill and every ounce of goodwill available was thoroughly tapped. After the Israeli military government closed the schools and universities, Palestinian teachers gave classes to students in private houses and apartments, and doctors offered free medical treatment. In support of the boycott of Israeli products, specialist agricultural advisors began distributing advice to families on how to raise fruit and vegetables of their own.

The strategy of the Intifada was resolutely innovative, a clean break with the tradition of armed struggle preached and practiced by the PLO for decades past. Through civil disobedience, it sought to build a mass movement and encourage certain forms of self-management. Communiqué after communiqué called for nonviolent actions, or at least for actions whose violent nature was limited.

DAILY LIFE UNDER THE OCCUPATION

Another important aspect of the Intifada was its ritual of sheer bravura. Masking the face with a *keffieh,* scrawling political slogans on walls, flying Palestinian flags, escaping the army's vigilance during curfews, distributing and reading NUC communiqués: all these things were strictly prohibited on pain of arrest. The idea was to create a daily series of acts of defiance whereby the people of the territories could stand up to the IDF and reaffirm the personality and the existence of the Palestinian nation. This affected the relationship between occupied and occupiers by giving the former a dignity that had been suppressed since the imposition of Israeli martial law. In this sense, the Intifada was a revolt against surrender and humiliation.[7]

Despite the privations and difficulties that accompanied their struggle and its repression, the very fact of mobilization gave hope to Palestinians. During this period, the inhabitants of the West Bank and Gaza gained fresh confidence in themselves. They began to view the future of Palestine in a resolutely optimistic light. Despite their structural weakness in comparison with Israel, they were displaying determination and even heroism—and they were proud of what they were doing. Women, young men, and countless ordinary people who had little or no connection with political militancy were all rising to the challenge.

Such was the case of Jane, a schoolgirl of sixteen. Jane was the youngest of five daughters in a Christian family, living in a comfortable house in a quiet area of Beit-Sahur, a few miles from Bethlehem. Her father was a foreman who made a good living working for Israelis on the other side of the green line between Israel and the Occupied Territories. He also spoke fluent Hebrew; prior to the uprising, his Israeli associates were often invited to his house as guests. Like her parents and her brothers and sisters, Jane was a supporter of George Habash's PFLP; the fact that the head of this left-wing faction was a Christian may have had something to do with it. Jane looked forward to a future of service to the Palestinian nation: "Unfortunately, we Palestinians have no airplanes. If we ever do, I'll be at the head of the queue to get a pilot's license." In the meantime, she belonged to a group of young people her age who were learning the *dabka*. The *dabka* is a traditional Palestinian dance for both sexes that demands good physical shape as well as agility, given that the dancers are expected to carry out a series of different leaps. Because it involved meeting with a number of other people, the *dabka* was forbidden by the Israeli military—which of course made it all the more popular. Thus not only was it a part of local folklore symbolizing Palestinian identity; to dance it was also an act of political resistance.

Occasionally, in defiance of their mother, Jane and her sisters went out to throw stones at the soldiers. Once Israeli soldiers came to order the head of the family to take down a flag hanging on an electric pylon in front of their house. Jane's father, Abu Lana,[8] refused point blank to do so, and as a result his identity card, which he needed to travel inside and outside the West Bank, was confiscated. He had to go to the headquarters of the local civil government and fight to get it back, which he eventually did, after paying a fine.

One winter evening the family was gathered at home, crouching around a heater and discussing a recent NUC communiqué. There was a rap at the door; Abu Lana had no time to answer before three soldiers burst onto the veranda leading to the living room. Jane's mother called out, "It's the army!," giving Jane just enough time to crush the illegal tract into a ball and slip it into her mouth. It took several minutes to swallow, while the soldiers inspected and searched every room in the house. They left empty-handed, though the boldness of Jane's elder sisters and their determination not to be pushed around almost caused a disaster.

In April 1992 the little town of Beit-Sahur was relatively calm; the political engagement of its people had waned somewhat, and the soldiers of the IDF were no longer present. The most visible signs of the continuing intifada were the closed shops in the afternoon and the absence of nightlife or anything happening after dark. At Abu Lana's house, the evenings were spent in front of the TV. Two of the girls were married, and one of these now lived in Amman, Jordan; the other had stayed on in Beit-Sahur. Some of the family had been unable to go to Jordan for the wedding because the father and one of the sisters had been refused an Israeli permit to cross the border. Now there were only three sisters at home. The eldest, who was studying to be a nurse at the University of Bethlehem, tried to renegotiate the amount of her pocket money with her father; the family was having real trouble adjusting to a steep decline in its living standards. While Abu Lana still worked in Israel and still earned a reasonable wage, the forty-day curfew imposed by Israel during the 1991 Gulf War had prevented him from going to work and had bankrupted his own small subcontracting firm. Umm Lana, his wife, could not make ends meet. She raged against the Israelis, but at the same time she felt that the young men coming out of prison were showing off a bit too much.

Early one April afternoon, news spread through Beit-Sahur that a university student had been shot by Israeli soldiers in the center of town. The student, whose name was Anton al-Chomal, had been hit in the stomach or the head—nobody was sure. Jane was worried: she knew Anton; his family was related by marriage to hers. Suddenly the bells of the church started tolling, and a muezzin-like message came over the municipal loudspeakers. A man's voice, half aggressive and half terrified, announced that comrade Anton al-Chomal had "suffered martyrdom" a few hours earlier. Jane burst out sobbing and ran with her sister to join the stream of neighbors rushing to the church. The building was packed, no longer a place of prayer and reflection but a seething mass of people, mostly young, shouting, weeping, and jostling. The priest had lost control of the situation. Some of the girls were standing on chairs, staring at Anton's lifeless corpse being carried along on a board by four shebab. When it was hoisted above the heads of the crowd, draped in the Palestinian flag, the din reached a crescendo. The dead boy's friends were hard put to keep their balance as they shoved their way gradually to the church door: it was a wonder the body didn't fall off. Outside, the cortege proceeded to the cemetery, accompanied by ritual chanting. "With our souls and with our blood, we will sacrifice ourselves for you, Anton."

The cemetery at Beit-Sahur was too small to contain all the people. Some stayed outside. Others pushed forward to be as close as they could to the graveside. Young men of twenty, shebab, friends, and fellow students, pressed forward passionately to kiss the martyr's cold cheeks and drape themselves over his body. Anton's family stood aside as if the son or brother they had known had vanished utterly behind the image of a political militant and popular hero. Jihad, a member of the PFLP like the dead student, clambered on top of a tomb and delivered an impassioned speech. In the name of the party, he paid homage to a fellow activist cut down by IDF bullets and exhorted everyone present to carry on the Intifada. One last time, Anton's body was raised high and shown to the people. The board he lay on was tilted upright; the crowd whistled and shouted. In the presence of death, all restraint was abandoned; everyone gave full vent to their emotions. Anton was finally buried, and the people made their way in groups back to his family's house, higher up in the town. On the way an Israeli jeep stumbled across the mourners, and the heavily outnumbered soldiers launched a few tear gas grenades before beating a hasty retreat. This scattered the crowd into running groups. Two bystanders passed out from the fumes.

Later, a vigil was organized. The women gathered inside, with Anton's mother and sisters; the men stayed in the street. For three days the people of Beit-Sahur lingered around the al-Chomal house to show their sorrow, their solidarity, and their support for the bereaved family. Political militants took a leading part in all this. They made speeches, marched in step like soldiers, hoisted Palestinian flags, and hung banners and pictures of the martyr. After a few days they were dispersed by Israeli troops. Stones were thrown, and the IDF retaliated with tear gas.

Jane was still weeping. Her elder sister finally shook her and told her to control herself. "Stop crying. People will gossip," she said.

PURITANISM AND SOCIAL REVENGE

The Intifada imposed its own strict moral order. Its leaders took the view that the behavior of individuals should conform to the principles and objectives of the political revolution. On this point, the nationalist and Islamist movements were agreed: before it could confront the enemy, Palestinian society had to cleanse itself. The potency of Palestinian nationalism depended on the vigor of Palestinian society. To revive it, the community of the Palestinian people had to be reinvented and restructured around traditional and religious values.

The ideology of resistance forbade any calling in question of the social order defined in this way, and it frowned on all forms of pleasure and amusement. In the view of the leaders and militants of the Intifada, it was vital to avoid dissipating valuable energy in futile distractions. The people needed to concentrate fully on the struggle ahead. As a result, night life was nonexistent. What cafés and restaurants there were stayed closed in the evenings. In the Gaza Strip, Palestinians were anyway obliged to abstain, since the Israeli Army enforced a permanent curfew between 9 p.m. and 5 a.m. each night. By day, family or school-organized excursions to Israel were a thing of the past, and the Gaza militants even forbade families to go to the beach. Everybody in the West Bank and Gaza adopted a Spartan way of life, either by conviction or by obligation. Marriages were celebrated with extreme discretion, and the dowry system, whereby a bridegroom was expected to spend large sums of money on a celebration, was condemned as retrograde. Such celebrations as there were, were halted any time a martyr was killed.

All this stemmed from a wish to build a healthy society, one that had rid itself of behavior viewed as socially reprehensible and religiously wrong. The revolutionary spirit of the Intifada had a strongly puritanical dimension. One of the arguments used to justify its moral rigor was purely tactical: people who contravened the moral order created a flaw in the wider community, one that could be exploited by the occupying power. A drunkard, a drug addict in need of his dose, or a young woman who defied sexual taboos were all easy prey for the enemy. The Israeli Army could take advantage of the weaknesses of Palestinians to recruit spies among them. The enemy, or those who collaborated with the enemy, could easily extract information from such people, and this fact served as a pretext for the shebab to maintain an iron grip on the workings of Palestinian society.

The values and norms endured by the people of the Territories for the sake of the Intifada have determined the course taken by an entire generation. For the most youthful participants in the uprising, or for their younger brothers growing up during this period, not to conform to the rules of strict traditional and/or religious morality was tantamount to political treason. Anyone who succumbed to the lure of sex or any other forbidden pleasure was suspected or accused of conniving with the Israelis. Even though these people might not have crossed the threshold of collaboration, they were viewed as being well on the way to doing so. Jihad, who led Anton's funeral march in April 1992, was caught in the arms of his girlfriend a few weeks after. Confirmed PFLP militant though he was, active at the university and a man who had spent time in an Israeli jail, he still received a warning through a member of his entourage: "Watch your step: you'll end up a collaborator."

But women, far more than men, bore the brunt of this moral pressure. In the Gaza Strip in the late 1980s, they were gradually corralled into wearing the veil. The movement began with a small number of women from poorer backgrounds, mostly living in the refugee camps. As the sisters, daughters, and wives of men killed, wounded, or imprisoned by the Israelis, they stopped using makeup or wearing pretty clothes as a spontaneous sign of mourning and grief. *This was no time for finery.* Progressively, in the working class areas that were most heavily mobilized for the battle with the Israelis, social pressures forced all women to cover their heads. The veil became a patriotic obligation, a uniform proclaiming that its wearer supported the Intifada. The contribution of the female sex to the purging of society was an essential one; the good conduct of a family's young women and wives was a proof of its honor.

Very quickly, women from bourgeois backgrounds gave in to the threats of the shebab, embracing the new rules of modesty and surrendering to the general Islamization of morals that had swept the Territories. Before long, any woman walking bareheaded in the streets of Gaza was liable to be insulted or stoned. Brutal intimidation quickly persuaded those few who resisted that they would have to obey the laws laid down by militant gunmen, who had no political training or experience but retained a monopoly on physical coercion.[9]

An awareness of the often hostile relations between social classes in Palestine is essential to any understanding of the Intifada. The political ambition of some militants reflected a repressed desire for social vengeance, insofar as compelling the bourgeoisie to adopt the behavior of ordinary conservative working people was a triumph and a vindication in itself.

When the first signs of trouble emerged, many members of the wealthier and more powerful Palestinian families were suspicious of this proletarian invasion—after all, the wealthier bourgeoisie was the traditional repository of political influence and had steadily increased its holdings in industry and real estate over the years. Economic muscle had enabled representatives of the various dominant clans to create broad networks of patronage among the general population. Some had occupied what might be termed an "interface position" with the Israeli military administration, negotiating various accommodations with it. The NUC broke with this line, excluding any possibility of cooperation with the occupying authorities. The NUC began by implicitly sidelining the traditional leaders of Palestinian society, in the sense that it claimed control of the armed struggle as well as of society's way of functioning. Thereafter it explicitly threatened those representatives of leading families who ventured to criticize the PLO or showed any kind of interest in the "Jordanian option." The latter was a plan endorsed by a section of the Israeli political class, which involved the West Bank's integration into the Hashemite Kingdom; it had won the favor of certain prominent Palestinian families in Nablus and Hebron. In general, these were people who had close political and economic ties to the Jordanian government and distrusted the PLO leadership.

With the exception of these few marginalized families, Palestinian society was firmly behind the objectives and actions prescribed by the NUC, and because of this the early stages of the Intifada were remarkable for their unanimity. The success of the mobilization was undoubtedly due to a temporary but strong alliance among the shebab of the working classes, the intelligentsia, and the commercial milieu.

The universities of the West Bank and Gaza were hotbeds of political agitation, with students and professors pouring out ideas and new militants every day. They made sure that the principles and procedures of the Intifada were spread through every level of the population. The faculties of Bir Zeit near Ramallah and Najah at Nablus brought together students from every conceivable social and geographical background: young men and women from the cities, the villages, and the refugee camps; rich and poor.

The commercial and shopkeeping classes made a significant contribution to the rising, merely by applying the NUC's directives. As a rule, this sector of society had tended to hang back; now they joined the nationalist cause. Trapped as they were within a system of constraints that regulated economic exchanges between Palestinians and Israelis, and bled white by a fiscal system that was heavily stacked against them, they had every interest in changing the rules. Thus the shopkeepers wholeheartedly participated in a boycott of Israeli products, observed strikes when they were called, and refused to pay taxes. Initially the shebab and the shopkeepers supported one another, and young fighters would come to repair the shopkeepers' steel shutters when they were damaged by Israeli troops. But before long the relationship began to go sour when

Nablus activists started looting shops on the pretext that their owners were failing to respect the boycott on Israeli goods.

A turning point was reached when the army finally broke the shopkeepers' resistance by forcing them to pay their taxes; this they did when their property began to be seized for debt. A rift now opened between the shebab, who had nothing to lose, and the middle classes, who needed to survive the devastating consequences of Israeli repression. The excesses and summary methods of some of the radical militants were beginning to cause outrage. After several years of privation, the population was drained; the fact was that the economic crisis brought on by the Gulf War had caused altogether too much hardship, and the collective élan and unanimity of Palestinian society had been shattered.

The petering out of the uprising can also be explained by the effects of the repression, which decapitated the movement by imprisoning or banishing its leaders. Bereft of its battle-hardened political leaders, the Intifada was taken over by younger and younger militants with progressively less experience. These men resorted all too easily to violence, including violence directed against Palestinian society itself. There were clashes between rival groups, with particularly savage competition between Fatah and Hamas[10] activists eager to carry off some spectacular coup. In some places, however, the activists appeared to be more interested in consolidating their local power than in fighting the Israelis.

The militarization of the Intifada accentuated these turf rivalries. Armed groups proliferated, as support money flowed in from the PLO in Tunis and Amman. The Palestinian central command, struggling to maintain control over the uprising, did its best to stay in contact with the militants in the field and provide funds for them, but it was itself sapped and confused by internal rivalries.

Probably it was to the advantage of the Palestinian leaders abroad to maintain a certain level of disorder in the West Bank and Gaza, with a view to weakening the emergent alternative power structure that had taken root in the Occupied Territories. The proliferation of armed groups tended to sow confusion, insofar as it was hard to identify activists because they were masked in public. Being armed, albeit lightly, the activists themselves found it all the easier to fall back on the use of force.

Thus the failure of the first Intifada was largely due to its protagonists' failure to articulate their nationalist and social aspirations. Young
people from poor backgrounds gave the movement its early impetus.
After 1990 they cut themselves off from the rest of society and fell back
on threats and brute force to prolong their movement's earlier unanimity. Nevertheless, their credit ebbed away. The civil resistance and limits
on violence that had been the Intifada's greatest strength now receded,
leaving a growing culture of brutality that chiefly worked against the
Palestinians themselves—for in the end Palestinians were the only ones
to suffer from the witch-hunts of real or imagined collaborators, and
from the gangsterization of activist groups.

THE INTIFADA ADRIFT

In the course of 1995, the final spasms of the Intifada shook Nablus.
The soldiers of the IDF and the Israeli settlers of the surrounding area
went unmolested, even though Israeli newspapers were taking a close
interest in events. A group from the working-class areas of the old town
decided to clean up Nablus and eliminate those elements it considered
harmful, notably collaborators and drug dealers. Three individuals were
executed, and ten more were shot and injured as a warning to others.
The gang responsible took full advantage of the Israeli Army's passive
attitude. At that juncture, the Palestinian Authority's takeover of the
West Bank cities looked to be just around the corner, and the Israeli
Army was no longer concerned to keep the peace in zones that it knew
were about to pass under Palestinian sovereignty.

Ahmed Tabuq was the head of the group that now occupied center
stage in Nablus, where events suggested that a certain number of shebab
might give considerable trouble to the Palestinian Authority, which had
come into being in 1994. These shebab, having been active from the
start of the intifada, had already founded and dissolved several suc-
cessive armed groups, variously named the Ninja Forces, the Black
Panthers, and the Falcons. In 1989 the Ninja Forces took the lead in
hunting down collaborators; some of them were arrested, and others
were shot down in the old city center by Israeli army commandos. A
year later the Black Panthers took over, as young men from the old town

center waged a campaign against Israeli agents and skirmished with groups belonging to Hamas, Fatah's Islamist rival.

In spite of the contacts and funds they received from outside Palestine, the shebab flatly disobeyed the directives of the PLO when it ordered them to stop executing collaborators. If they needed money, they addressed themselves to the wealthier citizens of Nablus. The bourgeoisie gave in to their demands, either because they were intimidated, or because this was the best way to secure some measure of protection.

Between 1990 and 1991, Ahmed Tabuq and his companions were all arrested and jailed for life, only to be given amnesty later under the terms of the Oslo accords when Palestinian autonomy was installed in Gaza and Jericho. The shebab were released on condition that they remained under Palestinian jurisdiction, meaning that the original gang from the old town of Nablus had now to live in Jericho, under the watchful eye of the Palestinian security services. It was out of the question for the nascent Palestinian Authority to imprison these "heroes" of the Intifada, and thus Tabuq and his friends escaped without difficulty, made their way home, recovered their weapons, and built up another group, the Falcons, which quickly won control over the medina of Nablus and its surrounding area. Tabuq himself, nicknamed the "Palestinian Rambo" by the Israeli newspapers, created something of a media sensation. His followers were all of very humble origin; none had stayed in school beyond the age of fourteen, and they were drunk with the power they wielded over the local population. In an interview, Tabuq claimed that his ultimate reference was "the people." "We are trying to promote the power of the people, for the people, and what we decide comes from the grass roots, in the absence of a Palestinian Authority here."[11] Nevertheless, Tabuq was ready to swear loyalty to Yasser Arafat, whom he recognized as the paramount leader.

To be fair, Tabuq's gang strongly identified with its community, and it strove to represent the deprived people of the old city of Nablus. In this way, even though these young men were allied with other Fatah groups like the ones in the refugee camps on the edge of Nablus, they nevertheless remained a distinct, self-sufficient faction. Their grounding and their popular approach set them on a collision course with the entrenched Nablus bourgeoisie.

Half a dozen families had controlled the political and economic life of the town of Nablus for over a century past. The position and authority of these few respected names also rested on a circle of people who were under obligation to them, as part of a system built up over the years as a form of social patronage. The sheriff's role that Ahmed Tabuq and his entourage wanted to fill had to be placed within the context of the social segregation and domination that were particularly strong in Nablus. The Fatah activists in the medina were more eager to punish members of their own society than to work for the liberation of all, and nationalist rhetoric legitimized this, though the initiative was obviously marred by a desire for social vengeance. It was no coincidence that the "enemies of the Palestinian nation" who were most under attack by the shebab nearly always belonged to the upper echelons of Nablus.

The group went on the offensive against its perceived enemies a few months prior to the end of the Israeli military occupation. The move was condemned by the Fatah organization in the city. Struggle against the bourgeoisie had no part in Fatah's revolutionary training program; on the contrary, the idea was to prevent the fragmentation of Palestinian society after the cessation of the war with Israel, amid the power struggles that would certainly follow. The career of Ahmed Tabuq seemed all the more dangerous because it looked very much as if the ruling families of Nablus had earlier used Tabuq and his like to commit crimes and settle personal scores. Secrets are well kept in Nablus; nevertheless, the shebab quickly became potentially troublesome witnesses for certain leading personalities in the city.

The story of Tabuq is instructive in a number of ways. For one thing, it shows why the first Intifada fell apart. In the absence of their natural political leaders, who had been neutralized by Israeli repression, the youngest militants took control of the movement and imposed their own crudely violent methods. In this way they wrecked the logic that gave credibility to civil disobedience, while at the same time deepening divisions within society. Moreover, coming just before the creation of Palestinian autonomy in the Occupied Territories, the shebab's demonstrations of force raised the question of submission to the new authority. How could leaders coming in from the outside consolidate power over these militants, as well as over the rest of society? The task was a tricky one. To start with, they were the promoters of a peace agreement with Israel, the terms of which were far below Palestinian expectations. Next, they had to convince the shebab to give up both their role and their status, at a time when the shebab were firmly convinced that it was their own decisive pressure that had brought the Israelis to the negotiating table in the first place.

CHAPTER TWO

Building Palestinian Autonomy, 1994–2000

The secret negotiations between representatives of Yitzhak Rabin's government and members of the PLO close to Yasser Arafat eventually yielded a project for Palestinian autonomy over certain areas of the Occupied Territories. The transfer of control over these territories to the Palestinian Authority was accomplished gradually, in several stages. The intermediary agreement was signed in Cairo on May 4, 1994; it constituted a first application of the principles concluded in Washington, D.C., on September 13, 1993. The Israeli Army evacuated the two zones, abandoning them to the first Palestinian forces that arrived to fill the vacuum. In truth, the Israeli authorities had come to view the Gaza Strip as totally ungovernable, and they were only too happy to relinquish this territory of 370 square kilometers with its restive, seething population of one million souls.

Gaza had no strategic value, no natural resources, and no religious or historic importance to the Israelis. The Jewish settlers in Gaza numbered barely five thousand; nevertheless, their settlements occupied one-fifth of the strip.[1] Yet to this day the Israeli Army maintains a presence in 40 percent of the territory to protect the settlers, the main roads, and the frontiers. The PLO has its own police entrusted with maintaining security over 60 percent of the Gaza Strip; it also controls Jericho, a quiet town on the West Bank. The Palestinian Authority is in charge of the daily business of education, health care, and housing. The Taba accord concluded on September 28, 1995, handed over five other West

Bank towns (Jenin, Tulkarem, Qalqilya, Nablus, Ramallah, and Bethlehem) equivalent to 3 percent of the territory and 20 percent of the population. This is Zone A, over which the Palestinian Authority has civil control and the power to maintain security.[2] The settlements, the roads skirting Palestinian towns built for the settlers, the military camps, and the areas defined by the Israelis as security zones—i.e., 73 percent of the West Bank—remained under Israeli sovereignty. The redeployments negotiated for the Wye River accords[3] brought about further transfers: 18.2 percent of the West Bank passed into Zone A, 21.8 percent into Zone B, and 60 percent remained under Israeli control. Interim arrangements[4] were designed to last five years. The thorny questions of Jerusalem, the Israeli settlements, and the Palestinian refugees were put aside. They would be discussed as part of the negotiations on the final status of the Palestinian Territories, planned for 1999. In the meantime, Israel maintained its control over the West Bank and Jerusalem, which it claimed as the indivisible and eternal capital of the Hebrew nation. In 1992, 120,000 Israelis were living in the settlements, and by 2000 their numbers had increased to 200,000. During Ehud Barak's administration, the number of settlements grew from 100 to 145. The PLO leader explicitly recognized the Jewish state and accepted the Israeli demands set out during the Oslo negotiations. In short, he contented himself with a politically and territorially limited autonomy—a massive concession for Palestinian nationalism, which even in its most moderate form had aspired to a Palestinian state with pre-1967 borders.

For Israel, this first stage represented the acid test of Yasser Arafat's ability to impose a new political order on his fellow Palestinians, while at the same time taking care of his own security.

The triumphant return of the PLO leader to Gaza coincided with the recovery of certain freedoms for the Palestinian populace. Their sense of relief was notably reduced, however, when it became clear that their liberation was incomplete. The Palestinian Authority, by recruiting large numbers of shebab from the Intifada for its security services, made an attempt to contain the violence while building a semblance of political order. In the Gaza Strip, a small territory but one with a certain degree of continuity, it succeeded in exercising fairly effective levels of control over society. In the West Bank, its power was limited to one or two enclaves and soon came up against a continuing Israeli presence.

Above all, the Palestinian Authority had to contend with local elites and the reality of class conflict. The bringing together of Palestinians from the outside, the taming of the shebab, and the integration or neutralization of local grandees was to prove a difficult and delicate exercise.

THE END OF THE GAZA OCCUPATION:
RELIEF FROM PRESSURE

In April 1994 the Israeli Army was still present in the Gaza Strip, though keeping a low profile. Since the handshake between Yitzhak Rabin and Yasser Arafat in Washington in September 1993, the day-by-day pressure exerted by the IDF had relaxed somewhat. All the same, the security services were still bent on the elimination of various members of Fatah's armed wing. At one checkpoint, an Israeli soldier tried to talk to a Palestinian driver, as if he hoped to leave the area with the memory of at least one positive encounter. "Are you happy about the peace?" But the man he stopped was disinclined to fraternize. "We'll be happy enough when you're gone" was the cold response.

The curfew that kept people inside between 9 p.m. and 5 a.m. every night was still being enforced. Tentatively the shebab began to defy it and to use certain streets that had previously been off limits. A growing sense of joy was beginning to pierce the gloom and bitterness left over from years of occupation. Then the first Palestinian police arrived in Gaza from the surrounding Arab countries. For some of the youngest, the sons of Palestinian refugees from 1948, this was their first experience of the Strip. They were warmly welcomed. Many of the people were relatives with whom they had been in close contact by phone or by mail, though they had never met. The ones who formed the lower echelons of the new civil and military administrations had often had a difficult time in exile, confined to refugee camps in Jordan, Syria, and Lebanon. They were leaving one camp for another, but at least this time they were in Palestine. Many a family in the refugee camps of Jabalya or Chati near Gaza City had to double up to make room for these newly arrived cousins. For the moment, hospitality was unanimous; indeed, the sudden arrival of armed and uniformed Palestinians provoked an outburst of unbridled joy. Israeli uniforms would soon be gone altogether. The photographers of Gaza were much in demand. Children and young people of both sexes, as well as grandmothers, posed proudly with guns borrowed from the Palestinian police.

Those Palestinians who had been banished by the Israelis a few years or decades earlier were authorized to come home. The return of fathers, prodigal sons, and companions-in-arms was feted by their families and the whole community. Canvas tents were erected in front of houses to receive the continual flow of visitors. Men hugged one another, giving four, eight, or twelve kisses to the militants whose exile had finally come to an end. Salvoes were fired in the air, in token of victory.

The generals of the IDF had decided to bring forward their departure by a few days, and to creep away by night, out of sight of the Palestinians. They need not have bothered. The transfer of power to the Palestinian police attracted a large number of young onlookers, who seized the occasion to exact a symbolic revenge. The rearguard of the occupation force was pelted with stones, whereupon the new representatives of Palestinian law and order orchestrated an outburst of collective exultation by firing their guns frenetically in the air for hours on end. The crowd, almost entirely made up of males, was in a state of frantic excitement. Amira Hass, a correspondent for *Ha'aretz,* the left-wing Israeli daily, chose this moment to inquire in Hebrew if there was anyone present among the shebab who spoke her language—to the consternation of a British colleague accompanying her. But to his surprise, several young men turned around, said "yes," and talked to her. The Israeli journalist calmly continued with her reportage.

Next, the curfew was lifted and the people of Gaza luxuriated in the pleasures of living by night as well as by day. Falafel sellers set up improvised tables outside, and the restaurants opened their doors. The steel barrels that had closed off so many of the city's streets vanished like magic. Along the seafront road, good-humored traffic jams testified to the people's yearning simply to go outside. The shebab made plans for nights on the beach under the stars; the women were soon nostalgic for the evenings when their men were locked up with them at home, but they were more than willing to exchange the terror of a sudden raid by Israeli troops—and the possibility that a husband or a brother might be dragged off to jail—for their present solitude. Even those who lived in the middle-class area of Rimal were sufficiently reassured by the presence of the Palestinian police to put aside their veils.

In the working-class areas of Gaza, the younger members of Fatah viewed the prospect of joining the police with considerable favor. The uniform was tempting in itself, and to take part in the building of a new Palestinian state under the command of their leader Yasser Arafat fit neatly with their careers as militants.

Nevertheless, the long-term implications of the agreements signed with Israel were not yet entirely clear. As a general rule, trust and loyalty toward the local and national leadership won the day. The relief people felt at seeing the backs of the Israelis and the achievement of a completely new level of freedom was bound to make them more than usually optimistic, but still certain questions remained unanswered. When would the prisoners come out of jail? What would be the fate of the Palestinian opposition? The idea that Islamists who had committed acts of violence against Israel might be surrendered to the Jewish state was quite unacceptable, even to those who were in favor of the peace process. Likewise, the continued presence of Israeli settlements in the West Bank and the Gaza Strip was a source of real concern.

Outside Arafat's immediate political circle, the sense of newfound freedom was shadowed by suspicion. Yussef, a resident of the Jabalya refugee camp and a partisan of the PFLP, saw the TV images of Palestinian police being trained in Egypt. "Why've they got night-sticks? There'll be nobody to beat but us!" was his angry comment. The setting up of an authority with a monopoly on physical constraint provoked a ripple of fear in a generation for whom institutional violence had always been closely identified with the illegal occupation of their country by the Israelis.

Journalists worried about the Palestinian Authority's likely attitude toward press freedoms. Word of Yasser Arafat's autocratic ways, and the known corruption of his Tunis entourage, had filtered through to Gaza. Nevertheless, doubts like these about the political future of the territories were not allowed to tarnish the welcome given to the head of the PLO. He was the father of the nation, the symbol of the Palestinian struggle, and he was acclaimed as a liberator as soon as he arrived in Gaza.

In Yasser Arafat's wake came the members of the PLO and their families. Some had shared years of exile with the "Old Man" (*al-Khtiar*) from the Gulf nations to Tunis by way of Jordan and Lebanon, and their families had never before set foot in Gaza. Between the local working people and these newly arrived bourgeois, there was a cultural collision.

The Gazans had had very few opportunities for exchanges with the outside world. Between 1949 and 1967, their enclave had been held in an iron grip by the Egyptian military administration: Cairo had never shown the slightest intention of integrating them in any way at all. Egyptian universities were closed to Palestinians from the area after 1970. The Israeli occupation cut them off even more from the Arab nations; and so, forced in on itself as it was, Gaza society remained deeply conservative. Economically backward, essentially agricultural, this corner of Palestine with its population of 80,000 then had to absorb a tidal wave of refugees in 1948, when no fewer than 180,000 Arabs of mostly rural origin took shelter there following the mass exodus brought about by the war. Today, in 2003, half the population still lives in insanitary refugee camps. The experience of Intifada has strengthened the people's loyalty to traditional and religious values.

The heads of the PLO, men who are close to Arafat himself or who are high-ranking military officers, have all had a taste of a rather different life. After seeing combat in Jordan and Lebanon, some of these had moved to North Africa, particularly Tunis, where they were able to live in relative comfort. Their way of life was paid for by the Gulf monarchies, and it distanced them from the precepts of the community in which they were born. Families that had lived abroad were immediately identifiable in the Territories by their obvious affluence, and by the fashionable European clothes of their women and children.

In general Gazans viewed the newcomers kindly, accepting the difference. In particular, there were "Arafat's children," the sons and daughters of PLO members killed in action, and for whom the PLO leader had assumed responsibility. These orphans all came to live in a dilapidated seafront building beside the road and for a while were the object of much interest and goodwill, despite their out-of-step style. But other Gazans were irritated by the newcomers of the diaspora. Young Islamists, in particular, viewed the Westernization of PLO members as a betrayal of the Palestinian nation. Rafat, for example, is a twenty-year-old electrician living in the Chati refugee camp. A Hamas militant, he thinks that the "foreign" Palestinians in Gaza "do harm to society. They spread debauchery. They drink, they have rowdy parties in the evenings. Many of their women have been parading around without veils ever since they arrived. They've turned away from Islam." The responsibility of these "troublemakers" seemed all the greater given that they occupied positions of power within the Palestinian Authority. Very quickly the population of Gaza began to call them "Tunisians," even though few of their number had ever actually lived in Tunisia. The nickname clearly showed how the newcomers were set apart by branding them as foreigners. It also defined their closeness to Arafat.

Not unexpectedly, the exiled Palestinians developed a few clichés of their own. Some were staggered by what they had come back to. For one thing, there were practically no amusements at all. There were only two or three decent restaurants, none of which served alcohol. And there were no clubs, cinemas, or theaters in Gaza. The returning exiles began to look down on the Gazans as backward primitives. Some openly showed contempt, or an arrogant desire to educate and reform local society. But despite these perceptions on either side, relations were not necessarily strained between the Gazans and the "Tunisians": neither formed a hermetically sealed grouping. Indeed, many shared the same family ties and had strong links of affection.

When they moved back to Gaza, the exiles had to resign themselves to being penned in just like everyone else. The ones in positions of power were able to move about more freely, traveling to the West Bank, Tel Aviv, or foreign countries as they pleased. Nevertheless, the Israelis regularly imposed a total blockade on the Gaza Strip, to prevent suicide bombings or in retaliation for them. Even the VIP cards of the bourgeois were no defense against the security measures decreed by the IDF.

Within a few years, the diaspora had made its mark on Gaza, creating its own meeting places and its own leisure venues. A section of the beach was cleaned up; bungalows were built and rented to holidaymakers. A chic restaurant, The Windmill, was opened, serving expensive meals and featuring lotteries and dancing in the evenings. This and a few other places preserved the tight social circle formed by the exiles and a smattering of Gazans linked to the networks of the Palestinian Authority.

TRAINING OF THE SECURITY FORCES

The first task of the Palestinian Authority, whose ranks were essentially filled by former exiles, was to give itself some kind of legitimacy in the eyes of the Territories' inhabitants. Were the shebab, who had won the struggle for power through the Intifada, ready to eclipse themselves, co-operate with their new overlords, and accept their methods? These were burning questions, all the more so because the young men of the uprising were convinced that the agreement signed by the PLO was a direct result of their campaign against the occupying forces, and of the pressures they had brought to bear on the Israelis.

The new regime could hardly congratulate itself on a decisive victory over Israel. The terms of the accord negotiated by the PLO fell well short of Fatah's aims. The moderate majority group among the Palestinian leadership was committed to establishing a Palestinian state within the pre-1967 frontiers, with East Jerusalem as its capital. The Oslo accords gave the Palestinians nothing but the bastard status of autonomy over most of the Gaza Strip and a small area of the West Bank: as a comprehensive formula for an enduring peace, its future was uncertain to say the least. Furthermore, the Palestinian Authority had nothing like the kind of revenue that might allow it to buy a measure of social peace and acquiescence to the new political order. The assistance supplied by the international community was a help, but it was always tied to the financing of specific projects.

The leaders therefore counted on a massive recruitment of young men from the Intifada to the armed forces, in order to consolidate their own power. In the Gaza Strip, this strategy of absorption seemed to work well. Access to the police profession or that of a regular soldier was always a viable alternative to unemployment or uncertain manual labor for a generation that had opted for political engagement at the expense of university or professional training. Moreover, by joining the apparatus of the Palestinian Authority, the shebab had the illusion of preserving some of the raw power that had been theirs hitherto. Being mostly members of Fatah, they naturally identified with their leaders and with the roles allotted to them.[5]

If the shebab police caused trouble, the security chiefs had a number of ways to rein them in, both financial and physical. The experience of Jamal is an example. During the Intifada, he was a member of the Falcons, the armed Fatah group. When the first police appeared in Gaza, he was of two minds. For the moment he obeyed his commanders, but he declared that in the future he might go over to Hamas if that formation showed itself better able to serve the interests of Palestine. Later, promoted to the rank of lieutenant in the military intelligence service, Jamal found himself involved in the repression of Hamas and Islamic Jihad. His views by then were very different. "If I was in charge," he said, "I'd get rid of the Islamists right away. . . . Frankly, instead of the Palestinian Authority I'd get together with the Israelis and occupy the Arab countries!"

MOBILIZATION AGAINST THE ISLAMISTS

Ahmed Jadullah works as a photographer for the Reuters agency. He is the eldest of seven children in a refugee family living in a Gaza suburb, and he is entirely self-made; though he is only in his mid-twenties, he has already won plenty of respect in his profession. Small and frail-looking, he appears gentle and sensitive. Using this, he has mastered the art of slipping unobtrusively into all kinds of situations, taking his photographs, and slipping out again. He has also proclaimed his independence from his father, a much-respected and devout figure in his part of town who preaches at the mosque from time to time on Fridays. The family is close to Hamas, though Ahmed himself is not a militant. He was jailed on one occasion, for no reason, during the Intifada: Israeli soldiers arrested him when they came to pick up his brother Salah, who was away at the time.

Salah had been an active militant ever since he saw their younger brother Khaled killed in an Intifada scuffle between soldiers and stone throwers. Khaled had taken a bullet wound: Salah went to help him, but Khaled told him to run so he wouldn't be arrested; the soldiers would make sure he got to the hospital. Nevertheless, Salah lingered on a nearby rooftop to see what would happen. Instead of helping Khaled with first aid, the Israelis riddled him with bullets while Salah looked on helplessly. From that moment, he became a committed militant.

One day in October 1994, Ahmed the photographer received a package at the Reuters Bureau, addressed to him by name. In it was a videocassette, which he immediately played. The image was not very clear: three young men, armed and masked, standing around another figure, a hostage. The three were Hamas commandos, and their victim was a kidnapped Israeli soldier, Nachon Waxman. The kidnappers claimed responsibility for the abduction and announced their conditions—freedom for all Hamas prisoners and notably for one of the movement's founders, Sheikh Yassine. Ahmed was profoundly shaken. The voice coming from behind the *keffieh* on the tape was one he knew well. It belonged to his brother Salah, the one the Israelis had come to arrest. Until that moment, Ahmed had known nothing of his brother's political and military activities, though he was only too aware of his anger against Israel.

The Israeli prime minister, Yitzhak Rabin, demanded that the Palestinian Authority apprehend Salah's Islamist cell. The intelligence services were convinced that the hostage-takers were somewhere in the Gaza Strip. Under heavy pressure, Yasser Arafat ordered his various security services to investigate quickly and expeditiously, and hundreds of Hamas operatives and militants were rounded up and interrogated. Ahmed, meanwhile, was still reeling from the discovery of his brother's involvement. He himself was thrown into a Preventive Security Service jail on suspicion of complicity. Meanwhile, the Hamas cell was located by cooperative intelligence work, not on territory controlled by the Palestinian Authority but in a village near Jerusalem under Israeli sovereignty. The Israeli leaders refused to negotiate and sent in an elite unit. The three kidnappers, after executing their hostage, were killed by the Israelis.

Ahmed heard this news while he was still in prison. The Israelis refused to give Salah's body back to his family. Ahmed was exonerated and set free, but now Gaza itself became his prison. Twice Reuters appointed him head of its Arab World Bureau in Abu Dhabi, and he was invited to Europe on several occasions to receive prizes for his photographic work. But Shin Beth, the Israeli interior security and intelligence service, remained unmoved. Ahmed Jadallah would continue to pay for his brother's crime, unable to leave the 370 square kilometers of Palestinian Authority territory.

The kidnapping of the soldier Nachon Waxman marked a turning point in the development of the Palestinian Authority's way of operating. Under Israeli pressure, the security services were mobilized to identify Islamist networks, interrogate suspects, and discover where hostage-takers were hiding. Surveillance and repression of Hamas and Islamic Jihad became the principal tasks of the Palestinian security forces, and the heads of the different services received substantial funds and used them to recruit more men. The Oslo accords had allowed for a nine-thousand-strong Palestinian police force; today the police number over fifty thousand. This huge increase was carried through with the tacit agreement of the Israeli authorities, because obviously the growth of a Palestinian police and intelligence apparatus contributed to Israel's own protection.

There followed a whole series of new offshoots, including a Civil Police Force, a General Intelligence Service, a Military Intelligence Service, a Preventive Security Service, and a Navy. There were also Force 17, the presidential guard, as well as the national security and special security forces. All of these operated within the autonomous zones of the West Bank and the Gaza Strip. As the structures proliferated, Yasser Arafat took advantage of them to distribute key posts to his allies and thereby to ensure their continued loyalty. By sharing out the use of force among several different leaders, he managed to avoid giving any one of them too much power. Divide and rule had always been the Old Man's favorite tactic. Nor were the jurisdictions of the security services all clearly defined, a situation that fostered intense competition among them. Their men were particularly visible in the Gaza Strip, where daily life was hampered by their endless interference. Before long the muddled initiatives of the younger recruits began to conflict with the flood of orders put out by senior officers determined to establish their authority over society in both Gaza and the West Bank.

THE REBELS OF NABLUS:
SCORE SETTLING AND CLASS STRUGGLE

In the months preceding the Palestinian Authority's arrival in Nablus, Ahmed Tabuq (the Rambo of the old town) and his friends negotiated with the new administration on the terms for their joining the security service. In December 1995, the Israeli Army pulled out of the city two days earlier than scheduled. The population flocked to the prison house; the Intifada militants among them were both excited and apprehensive about entering the building where so many of them had been interrogated, mistreated, and interned. The last activists emerged from hiding, were reunited with their families, and tasted their newfound freedom.

But this moment of respite was a brief one for Tabuq and his men. The Palestinian leadership, so accommodating only a few weeks earlier, had abruptly stopped answering their calls. The news was disturbing: apparently the Palestinian Authority now viewed them as outlaws, and there was even a rumor that certain highly placed figures favored eliminating them altogether. The *rais* (leader) demanded that the shebab surrender unconditionally; Tabuq and his four henchmen took fright and dropped out of sight. Next, the Palestinian police entered the old town and surrounded the house where they were hiding. After a two-day siege they surrendered, on the security officers' assurance that as soon as "one or two difficulties" had been ironed out, they could have jobs in one of the Authority's military organizations. In the event, Tabuq and his friends were to spend the next year and a half in secret cells without understanding why. They were reproached for failing to submit to Arafat's government, but no judgment on this was ever pronounced. Their jailers regularly told them that they would soon have a chance to present their case to the authorities. Yet the months went by and no interview was scheduled.

Other young men with ties to Fatah were targeted by the Palestinian security services. Nasser Juma and Mahmud al-Jemayel, two friends linked by a shared political militancy during the Intifada, had returned to peaceful civilian life after their release in April 1994. The former was an employee in a firm of mapmakers; the latter worked for an insurance company. Officially, the government accused them of instigating some of the actions of Tabuq's group. Nasser and Mahmud were obviously acquainted with the gang in Nablus; indeed, Mahmud's younger brother was a member of it. Nevertheless, Nasser swears that by the time the Palestinian Authority came into being he had given up all forms of armed struggle against the Israelis. It is true that his political maturity and his poise as a character bear little resemblance to the impulsiveness and brutal violence of Tabuq's group.

Having neutralized Tabuq, the Palestinian police demanded that Nasser Juma and Mahmud al-Jemayel surrender in their turn. Surprised and angry, the two men decamped as quickly as they could to Ramallah, a town due to remain under Israeli control for a few weeks longer. There they made an appointment to meet Fatah operatives from the General Intelligence Bureau. As soon as they arrived in the building they were arrested, their cell phones were confiscated and they were sent to join the other Nablus prisoners held in Jericho. After a few months they went on hunger strike, whereupon they were transferred to a jail in Nablus.

After two weeks without food, Nasser was greatly enfeebled. Left in solitary confinement, he fell at last into a deep sleep, but his Palestinian jailers refused to let him rest. "After an hour or so, they came and told me to get up. For a moment I thought they were going to put me in a more comfortable cell. Not a bit of it: they made me strip naked and stood me on a box. Then they tied my hands and beat me, ordering me to tell the story of my life. I just said I wanted to die. They hosed me down with water and beat me for several hours with lengths of electric cable. Eventually I passed out and they left me there. A little later, I heard Mahmud screaming. They were drinking *arak* (aniseed-based liquor). I've nothing against *arak*, but this was hardly the time or place for drinking. They were crazed, completely drunk. They were young guys, about our age, Palestinians from abroad. They must have hit Mahmud in the head. He lost consciousness and they took him to the hospital. I knew nothing about it. But after that their attitude toward me changed and they talked to me and took me out for medical attention. I saw some doctors. For five days I couldn't move, I was so badly hurt. I spent six months in jail after that."

Nasser survived, but Mahmud al-Jemayel died of his injuries. The news spread quickly and provoked fury in the working quarters of the town. The mosque was far too small to contain the huge crowd that turned out for Mahmud's burial. At the cemetery, the dead man's family had difficulty getting near his body, there were so many people pressing forward to embrace him. The funeral quickly turned into a gigantic demonstration against the Palestinian Authority. The mob trashed a gas station belonging to the mayor, Ghassan Shaka, and then marched on his residence.

The long and the short of it was that Ghassan Shaka, a prominent figure in Nablus, was deemed responsible for the death of Mahmud al-Jemayel, an Intifada militant from a poor family in the town. The shebab were convinced of his direct involvement. Among the local bourgeois, people were more circumspect, but it was understood that the mayor might have had something to do with the crime.

The Intifada militants speculated that Mahmud and Nasser could have had compromising information about Ghassan Shaka: proof, perhaps, that he had collaborated with the Israelis. There was also a rumor that al-Jemayel and Shaka had been in business together but had fallen out. Dr Muaiya al-Masri, a respected local figure and a member of one of the most prestigious families in Nablus, had been called in to examine Mahmud's lacerated corpse and had clearly testified that it bore the marks of torture. He went on record in condemning the vicious young thugs responsible, who thought themselves above the law. While the doctor did not go so far as to directly accuse Ghassan Shaka of arranging the torture session, he strongly suspected that the mayor had been involved in shady dealings with the two young men.

These suspicions were hardened by closer examination of Ghassan Shaka's family network. It now came to light that the mayor's daughter was married to the head of the local navy barracks, who was in charge of the prison in which Mahmud and Nasser had been held and tortured.

The Shaka clan is one of the leading families of Nablus. Since the early twentieth century, several of its members have occupied the post of mayor at the city hall. Others were successful in business, diversifying from original family landholdings into investments in industrial projects. Along with other families like the Masris, Kanaans, Nabulsis, and Abdelhadis, the Shakas had maintained their share of political and economic domination over the city since Ottoman times. In the nineteenth century, Nablus was already a manufacturing town specializing in textiles and soap making; each prominent family had its investments in the factories and preserved its own networks of patronage. Although there were rivalries among them, their members generally agreed on enough to protect their positions. To guarantee social order, they supported charitable activities on behalf of the city's poor.

During the period of Israeli occupation, some of the town's prominent citizens acted as intermediaries between the military administration and Palestinian society. The Israelis had a strong interest in supporting the power of the traditional elites in the West Bank and the Gaza Strip. Basically, these elites represented an alternative to the PLO, which Israel's leaders had ruled out as a possible negotiating partner right up to the 1990s. When Yitzak Rabin's government came to power in 1992, it discreetly broke the taboo by opening secret negotiations with PLO representatives. Furthermore, by preserving the status of local Palestinian notables, the occupying power gambled on their capacity to keep the political peace. After all, certain members of key families had shown themselves open to compromise when their economic interests were at stake.

But the coming of the Intifada overturned the social order run by the traditional elites. Their representatives were neutralized and marginalized by the militants of the uprising. Ghassan Shaka had problems with the shebab belonging to the Fatah organization, and the nature of the relationship was somewhat murky. Himself a member of Yasser Arafat's political apparatus, Shaka seems to have served as a courier moving PLO funds into the hands of the Intifada activists. Money may have been extorted from him during this period, and he may even have negotiated informal arrangements with some of the shebab. Secrets like this are very carefully kept in Nablus. Nevertheless, it is a matter of certainty that working relationships were formed between the two sides, shaped by power rivalries, class resentments and tactical alliances. Nasser Juma claims that at one time Shaka was heavily obligated to him. "During the Intifada, Ghassan had to wait for months before he could speak to us." Najy, without going into detail, adds: "I got on very well indeed with Ghassan Shaka—after I torched his car."

So the death of Mahmud al-Jemayel, Fatah militant, probably was not planned by the Palestinian Authority. The torture was merely carried too far, exceeding instructions. Yet the scenario whereby a group of unscrupulous and inexperienced underlings simply lost control of themselves holds no water. The decision to inflict physical pain in this case was taken by men well entrenched in the network that held power. The goal was to intimidate, to enforce silence, and to break the will of the two shebab. Clearly, Mahmud and Nasser had dangerous knowledge or represented some kind of direct threat to the reputations and interests of influential personalities.

This is no mere anecdote linked to the chaotic setting up of a new political system. Instead, it accurately reflects the inveteracy of class conflict in the town. The destabilizing rise of the shebab during the Intifada, followed by the return in force of the old dominant elite on the coattails of Palestinian autonomy, were real phenomena that reached their paroxysm at Nablus. In consolidating his power over the West Bank, and especially in Nablus, Yasser Arafat was unable to circumvent or swallow up the elite families. Yet the prestige and the solid support enjoyed by these people, and their close political and economic links with the Hashemite monarchy in Jordan, obliged him to be circumspect in his dealings with them. The "Jordanian solution" of assimilating the West Bank into the neighboring kingdom still had its partisans in certain Palestinian and Israeli milieus. The PLO leader had to prove to skeptics that his own government was the only possible solution. For this reason he reserved a number of important posts in his nascent Palestinian Authority for members of the traditional elite families of Nablus. He chose Ghassan Shaka as mayor, Maher al-Masri as minister of economy, Mahmud al-Aloul as governor, Said al-Nabulsi as head of the Chamber of Commerce. On their side, the notables used their own resources to ensure that they would not be dislodged either by Yasser Arafat's political system or by his military apparatus.

In this balancing act, Ghassan Shaka was a crucial player. As representative of a patrician family that had already supplied several mayors to the locality, he was considered to be close to Yasser Arafat. Shaka's ability to maintain two rival legitimacies in a state of coexistence, to hold the central power apparatus within bounds that the local elites could accept, was quite remarkable. Yet this compromise between powerful men worked to the disadvantage of the Intifada shebab from the working class. Tabuq's group was the all-around loser: its members were imprisoned for eighteen months without bail, an awkward witness was murdered, and the militants from the refugee camps were effectively neutralized.

When they came out of prison, Tabuq and his friends were offered jobs in the security services. The policy of bringing the shebab into the fold was in no way called into question by the "accident" of their incarceration. Two of them eventually joined the preventive security force but were quickly expelled for lack of motivation and zeal. In the end the original five all found themselves unemployed, purposeless, and without a future.

The ideological beliefs they shared were simply not strong enough to keep them together. Their version of the Palestinian struggle was no longer sustainable. With no political or professional plan, and shaken by their experience of repression, the shebab lost the direction that had formerly united them. Meanwhile Ghassan Shaka, seeking to consolidate the foundations of his power, was eager to defuse any opposition or potential disorder that might reoccur. In 2000 he offered work to Tabuq's men. Two of them accepted and became his bodyguards, on a salary of $300 per month. The mayor of Nablus had found a neat way to protect himself from unfriendly individuals, while procuring a brand new set of allegiances. One of the recruits explained his decision as follows: "Shaka is useful to Palestine and he has good contacts. He's a well-known figure, too." Thus, despite the conflictual aspect of the relationship, the idea of connecting oneself to a member of an influential clan remained an attractive, reassuring option for shebab who were at loose ends. Even though a former activist might have trouble getting up in the mornings or being punctual and regular at work, he would view his choice as giving him the framework he needed, and above all as a way to avoid "having problems."

Mahmud al-Jemayel's younger brother, another member of the group, prefers not to dwell on his former comrades' treachery. Today he is unemployed and powerless to influence events. He describes his state as follows: "When I got out of prison they offered me a job in the security services, exactly the one I'd wanted. But I turned it down. People like us will always be poor. We have no future. The bosses in the Authority say we're thugs, but the people know who we are and how we operate. They know the difference between honest, patriotic men and the other kind. When we were running Nablus, there was real justice. None of this stuff like alcohol and prostitution existed like it does now.

These days, you can see kids as young as fourteen drinking openly in the streets." The shebab who are now outside the new political order have no real way of opposing it.

THE TRIUMPH OF THE TRADITIONAL ELITE

Thus some, but not all, of Fatah's militants were absorbed into the new political system. As veterans, their new role was to maintain security; in this way they played their part in preserving an order that worked in favor of the middle-class business sector in Nablus. The local shop-keepers and entrepreneurs, whose work and projects had been seriously hampered during the first Intifada, were all for peace in the town; they opposed any major interference from the central power. Neutralizing the protests of the shebab was a sure way to ensure the comfort of the bourgeoisie.

Khaled, a case in point, was succeeding in business. The scion of a respected family in Nablus, he had joined his father's firm, which held a concession from a foreign car manufacturer. Khaled himself was in charge of developing the spare parts sector, selling throughout the West Bank. He had studied previously at the American University in Cairo, where he won the equivalent of a master's degree. All this was paid for by his father, and Khaled came back to Nablus when the Palestinian Authority was just moving in. He went to live with his family, rediscovering his father's paternal authority and his mother's smothering care. For as long as a young man from Nablus remained unmarried—and especially if he belonged to the middle class—he had to live under his father's roof. Exchanging one's freedom for the warmth and comfort of home is only a good idea up to a point. Khaled was thirty-three, the eldest of two sons and a daughter: discreet but persistent pressure was exerted on him. The former Cairo student yielded to it and began looking around seriously for a wife. This he found hard at first, but he was well aware of the advantages to be gained from belonging to a family that was "respected." If he followed the rules, he could count on the people around him in both personal and business matters. By behaving impeccably, he remained on course to inherit the prestige of his father's name. Khaled's family had an informal motto: "No politics, no standing out in a crowd, no excess." They would never compete with the Shakas, Masris, and Kanaans of their world. They didn't want to be mayors, members of Parliament, ministers, or chairs of the chamber of commerce; instead, they placed their trust in economic success and social standing. They studiously avoided being eccentric or defying the prevailing local mores.

Meanwhile, Khaled became aware that the behavior of his family had altered. When he looked through the photo album, he saw pictures of his mother and aunts in short skirts, whereas now they covered their hair with veils. His younger sister, working as a psychologist, wore the same clothes, and his younger brother was firmly on a course set by his elders. Only the youngest son defied the family and opposed their father's decrees. This son, Ayman, now aged nineteen, had been a child at the time of the first Intifada. When he was ten, his determination to take part in acts of resistance came up sharply against the will of his parents. Like the rest of his generation, which came of age in an atmosphere of violence, Ayman was far from obedient. His brothers were amazed: although they were older, they still dared not cross their father. Ayman became a Hamas militant and was sentenced to fifteen months in prison by the Israeli authorities. In the course of a trip organized by his school in 1998, he was intercepted and arrested at an Israeli Army checkpoint outside the zones controlled by the Palestinian Authority. Ever since, he had been forbidden to leave the Territories and was forced to complete his studies at the Nablus university, giving up the private faculty in Amman that he had formerly attended. In any case, Ayman preferred to stay in Nablus to accomplish what he perceived to be his duty as a Muslim and a Palestinian. "Trips abroad weaken one's political determination," he proclaimed, in a swipe at his brothers.

Khaled's uncle was a member of a charitable association, the *zakat* committee,[6] which gave assistance to about five thousand families in Nablus. Traditionally, the money came from generous foundations in the Gulf states. But since the summit against terrorism held at Sharm-el-Sheikh in 1996, funds from abroad destined for private organizations had been prohibited. Officially it was thought that organizations of this kind were being used to channel cash to Islamist movements. So the directors of the Nablus *zakat* committee took their own precautions. They feared a crackdown on their finances by the Palestinian Authority and reacted by investing the funds in profit-making ventures. They continued to give to the poorest people in the community and to pay the wages of employees in their cooperative organization.

Although Khaled had stayed away from politics on his return from Egypt, he made no secret of his opposition to the new administration. Yet the Palestinian Authority handled the traditional Nablus elite with kid gloves, to the point where they had recovered their position and status of pre-Intifada days. Broadly speaking, entrepreneurs had been able to run their businesses without interference from the Authority, which had treated the businesspeople of Gaza very differently. Despite that, the leading families of Nablus viewed the new ruling class of the PLO and the exiles with deep mistrust. They thought them ineffectual, corrupt, and arrogant, and they dreaded what might happen if there were an alliance between the leaders of the Authority and the militants of the uprising. The creation of the new security services was palpable proof of the links between the two groups. In the view of the middle class, the shebab of the Intifada, now metamorphosed into police, would exploit their new power to the hilt. Khaled tells this story: "My cousin intervened when a policeman stopped a woman he knew. The officer lost his temper and took him back to the station—and on the way, in a few minutes, the cops beat him up, just like that, for nothing. Sometimes you feel they're just itching to have a go at you."

And yet the security services are relatively discreet in Nablus. It is nothing like Ramallah or Gaza, where you will see official cars go by at full speed with flashing lights, with the drivers leaning on their horns at the slightest slowdown. And spot checks in the Nablus streets are rare. The power of the police apparatus is kept under wraps. The personality and status of Ghassan Shaka have made it possible to contain the unruly behavior of the new recruits, as well as their leaders' appetite for power. Other prominent men in the city may also have their share of influence over the new power networks.

This analysis is confirmed by an entrepreneur in Nablus, who has this to say: "Shaka's a good mayor. He keeps the security services under control. Sometimes he even knocks them about physically, but he's right—they're like animals and that's all they understand. Personally I despise the Authority guys who come here just to grab money. They want to turn us into their employees, or maybe their slaves. One time, somebody from the Ministry of Industry came to Nablus to make a speech about the government's support for entrepreneurs. I stood up and said we didn't want anything from them: no money, and no support either. We just wanted them to leave us alone. Before my company even opened for business, they were asking me to pay tax." But this man seemed to be earning plenty of money. Like everyone in the economic sector, he had done well out of the lowering of the tax on companies. During the Israeli occupation, this had stood at 38 percent; the Authority brought it down to 25 percent.

Between 1996 and 2000, the shebab of the Intifada were gradually assimilated into a social and political order orchestrated by the leading families. Through the charity organizations the latter controlled, they were able to soften the discontent of the poorest sectors of society. The town's mayor contrived to make the Palestinian Authority's new system coexist with that of the local bourgeoisie. Nevertheless, from prudence or necessity, Ghassan Shaka maintained no fewer than ten permanent bodyguards. Class conflict might be under control, but the potential for confrontation was and is still there, just beneath the surface.

THE SHEBAB—TORN BETWEEN RESENTMENT AND THE NEED TO IMPROVISE A LIVING

The heroes of the Balata refugee camp, Najy, Bassam, and Sami, were condemned to exile in 1992 and sent home at the close of 1995. On the way they were interviewed by the Israeli intelligence services, who demanded guarantees that they would renounce all forms of combat against the Jewish state. The three were in favor of the peace agreement, by which they would be amnestied. As militants, they trusted their leaders and approved their political choices. All three were offered jobs in the Palestinian Authority's security services. Bassam was recruited by the General Intelligence Bureau and Najy by Preventive Security. Sami did not want to join any police force, declaring that the military life was not for him. "I don't like discipline, and I hate getting up early in the morning. That kind of work isn't my thing." Instead, he got a job with

Fatah, "organizing activities." What he actually did was rather vague, but at least it yielded a monthly wage.

From the leaders' point of view, maintaining bonds of dependence like this made it possible to keep some kind of control over a few of the shebab from the Intifada. In addition, Sami signed up at the university, though he hardly ever went to classes.

It was not long before Bassam and Najy had second thoughts. Bassam resigned from the police the day he was ordered to repress militants from Hamas. In 1996 he signed up for a sociology course at al-Najah University in Nablus. "I thought it was time to do something on my own behalf," he says. His idea was to get a master's degree, leading to a job at the Social Affairs Ministry, or perhaps in a United Nations development agency. Above all, he wanted to study in Europe—more particularly in Italy, a country that had always attracted him because in his eyes the Italians were more sympathetic than others to the Palestinian cause. Yet Bassam knew that the Israelis would never authorize him to leave the Territories. Like most of his fellow shebab from the Intifada, Bassam was deprived of all freedom of movement, either to Israel or abroad.

Najy, given the task of interrogating Israeli agents, took a harder line—until a member of Hamas under his surveillance accused him of collaborating, at which point he immediately resigned. He moved to the civil police, where he concentrated on ordinary misdemeanors and common law crime.

At the same time, he was conducting a private investigation of his own at the university—looking for a woman with an education. He eventually met Leila, a Nablus girl studying for an accounting diploma. The two went out together and decided to marry, despite their social differences. Leila belonged to a good Nablus family; her father owned a small factory, and her mother came from a wealthy Jerusalem background. Najy was a native of the Balata refugee camp; he had never studied, and from being an armed Intifada militant he had graduated to a job as an ordinary policeman. Leila's parents had no objection: they were willing to accept their daughter's choice. But Leila's maternal uncles were strongly opposed to the match and went so far as to threaten their niece's suitor. Najy, the child of a refugee family, had his own way of conducting an argument. He jumped in his car, drove around to the uncles' house and sprayed it with bullets. His own relatives were against the marriage, too, on the grounds that mixing with the town's bourgeoisie would lead to trouble. Najy paid no heed; in any case, he had lived away from home since he was thirteen. He covered his new wife with gold, proving that he had the means to give her a good life. "My wife's relatives can't say a thing because Leila lives more comfortably with me than she ever did with them. I make good money."

The couple moved to Ramallah, where Leila was very happy. She felt freer than she had in Nablus, a thoroughly austere and conservative town. Ramallah was livelier, with fewer social barriers since the town had absorbed a significant proportion of migrants from the interior. Its dynamism in the industrial and services sectors made it an important economic center. Bir Zeit University, only fifteen kilometers away, attracted students from the West Bank and Gaza and made for a concentration of the intellectual elite. Some of the structures of the Palestinian Authority were based there, the rest being in Gaza. The arrival of the administration had provided a number of extra job opportunities, while many of the members of the Authority who had come with Yasser Arafat also came to live in Ramallah, as soon as they could decently get out of Gaza. And Palestinians from other towns, who had obtained jobs as civil servants, were not slow to follow.

Ramallah, twenty kilometers from Jerusalem, was the most Westernized place in Palestine. Its restaurants and bars were filled with people from all walks of life. You could have a beer or a glass of wine while listening to music; you could even dance. Young people walked about in oversized, falling-off jeans and back-to-front baseball caps. Styles like these caught on among the more affluent through the influence of the Palestinians from abroad or of Americans passing through or returning to the town.

Families from Ramallah had emigrated to the United States ever since the early twentieth century. The movement began with the Christians, and the Muslims followed. Some of these American families came back only for holidays, while others kept a foothold in their native town. Furthermore, a part of the diaspora that had left in the late 1990s from towns and villages now in Israel had returned to live in Ramallah, where the population was a blend of Christians, Muslims, villagers, refugees, and townspeople. There had always been a good understanding there between the Peoples of the Book. At the close of the seventeenth century, Christian families specializing in metallurgy and the timber industry exchanged the fertile lands they owned with Muslims who were prepared to work them. A strong Christian presence that lasted until the mid-twentieth century had also contributed to the town's relatively liberal outlook.

The Ramallah region had the highest proportion of refugees living outside the camps. It also housed a small minority of Palestinians from the surrounding towns and villages. Families born and bred in the town were by now a small minority, representing less than 20 percent of the total population. This change made Ramallah a place where people's anonymity was better preserved than elsewhere in the region. Likewise, society's control over people's behavior was not as stifling as it was elsewhere in the Territories.

At Bir Zeit University, veiled female students studied side by side with girls wearing the latest American or Israeli fashions. In one of Ramallah's bars on Saturday nights, an Israeli jazz band entertained the local crowd. The singer lived in a local Jewish settlement.

But in the end, despite his wife's objections, Najy resolved to leave Ramallah and go back to Nablus. His friends wanted him around, and friends like his were hard to get away from. So he rented an apartment in a residential part of Nablus and his wife found a job as an accountant. She gave birth to two little daughters. While Najy was able to provide them with material comforts, he was less able to give emotional stability and security. He was inclined to shout and lose his temper; he could be extremely brusque with his spirited daughters. He had been behind bars when each was born, condemned by the Palestinian Authority for violent acts he had committed. The first time, Najy had an angry argument with a member of a security service, after which he reverted to his old ways and let off steam by riddling the man's office walls with bullets. The second time, he threatened a wealthy entrepreneur who had invested money in Nablus.

Even so, after his spells in prison, the hero of Balata was given back his uniform and his police-issue sidearm. Although Najy was a headache to his superiors, the best way of neutralizing him was to keep him in his job. He could imagine no other profession; yet it is hard to say whether he was resigned to the status quo or was simply biding his time. His analysis was a harsh one: "From the British mandate onward, Nablus was run by its leading families. All that changed with the Intifada: children ruled the streets, and we had direct access to Abu Ammar by phone. When the Authority took over, everything was like before, and the leading families got their power back. Ordinary people had done the fighting, while the bourgeoisie reaped all the benefits. Of course Arafat surrounded himself with those people because he was under pressure from abroad, from Jordan and Egypt."

Like the vast majority of Fatah's partisans, Najy did not hold the head of the Authority directly responsible for his plight. As far as he was concerned, Arafat made mistakes because he had bad advisors and too little room for maneuver. The militants within Palestine tried to reassure themselves with the idea that basically, despite appearances, Abu Ammar was on their side. For the moment the image of the father of the nation could not be tarnished. What else was there to believe in?

Najy and his friends felt that the government had given in to profiteers and opportunists. To avenge an injustice, or to make a little extra money, they had plenty of imaginative ploys. Najy's police job brought in the equivalent of U.S. $270 a month. Since he was under the protection of Marwan Barghuti, a Fatah representative in Ramallah, he could count on an extra $500. Now the former fugitive wanted even more: he felt, understandably, that he had given enough to the cause to expect a few material advantages today. So now he was in business as well, helping his brother run a brisk trade in cars stolen inside Israel. It was highly profitable, because demand and supply were both consistently high. The vehicles were snatched by small groups of young men and sold in the West Bank just as they were, or broken up for spare parts. At the same time Najy discovered a passion for computers. Despite his rudimentary English, he learned quickly how to shop on the Internet—and how to operate credit card frauds.

Najy still had ways of profiting from his relationships with a certain category of the new Palestinian middle class. When somebody defaulted on a debt, certain unscrupulous businessmen turned to armed youths who were prepared to do what was necessary to recover the money. Najy knew a furniture dealer who required this service from time to time. He received 30 percent of the proceeds he extorted; at the same time he negotiated a 50 percent discount for his friend Sami's new bedroom furniture. It's hard to know exactly what it was that linked the affluent shopkeeper and the newly appointed policeman. Mutual interest, maybe. Perhaps a fascination with moneyed ease for the one, and a strategy for ensuring protection for the other.

All the same, doing business with the bourgeoisie was a far cry from actually liking them. "I don't like the bourgeoisie. My father paid for my uncle's medical studies. When he died, my uncle did nothing for us, and he didn't help when we were in prison, either," was Najy's bitter comment.

The social tensions built into the town of Nablus explain the violence of its class relationships. Although the shebab were generally under control there, there were many who nourished deep resentments and a desire for social vengeance. The Palestinian entity remains full of such latent conflicts among its various social groups. The Authority has attempted to bring every layer of the population into the apparatus of power, while itself holding the balance. Today its hold on society is due more to the special compromises made by the *rais* (leader) with certain individuals and groups than to the building of a durable framework of national representation.

CHAPTER THREE

Fault Lines among the Palestinians

The renunciation of the struggle with Israel and the forming of their own autonomous entity forced the Palestinians to confront themselves. The fight against the occupation had required that divisions be put aside for the duration, but the establishment of a system of power in the Territories changed existing *rapports de force* and created new tensions. Although Yasser Arafat had contrived to impose his authority on the population of the West Bank and the Gaza Strip, social and political divides were growing ever deeper, and this became uncomfortably obvious as the economic situation worsened.

Several phenomena reflected the logic of resistance that had made the Palestinian political community so fragile. Indeed, under the pressure of rejectionist attitudes, its contours became thoroughly blurred.

From the start, the Palestinian Authority had to face the basic challenge of preserving some kind of unity among the different fragments of territory it controlled. The handicap imposed by the absence of any territorial continuity was all the more crushing in that the movement of people and goods between the two portions of autonomous Palestine remained dependent on the good will of Israel. The sheer difficulty of keeping the West Bank connected to Gaza steadily diminished exchanges between their respective populations. Furthermore, Israel's policy for controlling the Territories made a deliberate distinction between the two areas and tended to give them different status. The growing distortions and de facto gulf between the two societies made each perceive the other in a negative light, and this was less than helpful in terms of national unity. In concrete terms, this gulf is manifested by a condescending attitude on the part of West Bank people toward those of Gaza, whom they view as hidebound and ill-educated. The arrival of young police from Gaza to join the service in Ramallah or Nablus provoked something approaching outrage. Among the many charges leveled against these interlopers by the townspeople of the West Bank was a tendency to look at their women altogether too closely.[1]

Other tensions were perceptible between the Palestinians who had stayed behind and those who had been forced abroad. The PLO members returning from exile shocked ordinary Palestinians, while their self-assurance and importance in the new hierarchy irritated some of the local notables who themselves aspired to power.

People's political postures reflected these deep social divisions, and the clearest rift of all was that between townspeople and refugees. Living in a camp was bound to trap individuals in a dismal socoeconomic milieu, and the fact of belonging to it gave them a specific political identity.

Lastly, the strategic options of the Palestinian administration tended to exacerbate such differences. Hamas, along with several other organizations, had declared its outright opposition to the Oslo accords and the autonomous regime. By carrying out attacks on Israeli civilians, the Islamist movement challenged the monopoly on "legitimate" violence that had hitherto been the sole property of the Palestinian Authority.

Yasser Arafat was subjected to contradictory pressures and imperatives. Israel was demanding that he dismantle all military political and social networks linked to the Islamist movement. At the same time, the repression of Hamas by his security services was obviously endangering national cohesion.

These spatial, social, and ideological divisions reacted with one another and grew harder and harder to manage. Were the existence of a political class and the setting up of a system of representation sufficient in themselves to give Palestinian society the means to grapple with its inner conflicts? Democratic institutions should provide a framework for organizing and orchestrating debates among individuals and groups. The recognition that differences exist, their public expression, and the discussion that should follow have a single objective: the removal of violence from politics, wherever it may originate.

THE REFUGEES OF THE CAMPS

The 1948 war drove hundreds of thousands of Palestinians into exile, and the refugee camps set up in its aftermath were intended as temporary shelters. The families that crammed into the first tents provided by the International Committee of the Red Cross came mostly from rural areas. They had been driven from their land, meaning they had lost all their capital. In 1950 the United Nations Relief Work Agency (UNRWA) took the place of the Red Cross, building barracklike concrete structures with corrugated iron roofs in place of the tent cities. The UN agency's directive was to improve the educational, socioeconomic, and sanitary conditions of Palestinian refugees in the West Bank, the Gaza Strip, Jordan, Syria, and Lebanon. It set up schools and training centers, and today, fifty years later, it continues to run dispensaries and provide food relief for the poorest families. UNRWA was supposed to be wound up as soon as the refugee problem was resolved. Despite the arrival of the Palestinian Authority, it remains responsible for the twenty camps in the West Bank and the eight along the Gaza Strip to this day.

HEAT—AND SUFFOCATION

The Chati refugee camp, or "beach camp," lies north of Gaza and extends for several kilometers along the Mediterranean shoreline. Sand invades the narrow alleyways between its tightly packed buildings. Here the population density is staggering: eighteen thousand people per square kilometer. A few streets have been laid out to allow vehicles to move through—to begin with, these were not so much urban planning initiatives as military imperatives. In 1971 the Israeli Army was directed by Ariel Sharon to create broad roadways into the camps, flattening about two thousand houses. The goal was to crush the movement of civil disobedience and guerrilla warfare that had sprung up along the Gaza Strip in the late 1960s.[2] The main arterial road crosses the Chati camp from north to south. A market is held each morning on the main square, adjoining one of the five mosques. A vacant lot in the center of the camp, formerly used as a soccer pitch, has been turned into a plaza. Further on, in the main street, stands UNRWA's primary school; twice a day, regular as clockwork, a flood of children in striped smocks spills from its gate into the street. The schools of the camp do not have the means to receive all the children at one time, and for this reason half of them go to class in the morning, the other half in the afternoon.

In Gaza, the camps look like slums. Prior to 1996, only 15 to 30 percent of the streets were asphalted; in the winter, people had to make their way through muck and great pools of stagnant water, while all year round drivers lurched along the rock-strewn tracks as best they could. Most houses are not connected to the primitive open sewage system, which leads straight into the sea; there are no recycling plants. Mounds of domestic refuse lie about everywhere; the housewives may insist on perfect cleanliness within, but they don't hesitate to toss their garbage straight into the street, where there are no garbage collectors to clean it up. Despite all this, residents express a strong attachment to the camp, in which most of them were born and raised; they are proud of belonging to its strong community. "We're simple people here, we have real affection for one another. It's different down there in Rimal[3] where there's money. Only simple people can love each other as we do."[4]

The houses are cramped, with insanitary lavatories and washing facilities. They usually consist of three or four rooms only, which are home to about a dozen people. Many of them still have their original corrugated iron roofs, which offer scant protection from winter cold or summer heat. The hovels in the streets are supposed to let in the light of day, but most of them, lost in the tight maze of construction, remain darkened—all the more so because their windows are usually tiny openings with shutters, set high in the walls to protect the household from prying eyes. Some of the residents have reproduced the traditional Arab house by building inner courtyards.

Abu Jamal's house is almost a pleasant one, thanks to the patio with a gnarled old tree in the middle. From the month of March onward, his sons come there with their friends to talk over a glass of tea or coffee. Each of his two younger sons occupies one room, with their respective wives and three children. Abu Jamal is a widower now, and he sleeps on a mattress laid out on the floor of another bedroom. There is a fourth room, shared by everybody, where guests are received and meals are eaten, spread out on newspaper on the floor. Ibrahim, the youngest of Abu Jamal's eight children, never studied and is now a sublieutenant in the Military Intelligence force. He is married to Salma, who is ten years younger than he but the oldest of five girls in a family that came to live at Chati on its return from Jordan in 1994. Salma left school at fourteen to marry Ibrahim, and since then she has presented him with three rambunctious sons. She seldom leaves the house: from time to time Ibrahim takes her in a car to visit her family a few hundred yards away, at which time Salma puts on her veil and a long tunic to hide her clothes. She has no female friends, knows almost nobody at Chati, and never goes out alone. And even if her husband would let her, she would not know which direction to take, or how to take a taxi. She is resigned to all this and makes no demands, yet she does not appear submissive at all. She has real authority over her children, in contrast to her husband, who when he's at home is quite incapable of controlling them.

Abu Jamal's two daughters-in-law have quarreled and do not speak to one another. So Salma spends most of her time penned up in her bedroom with her three sons, who would much rather run about and fight other boys outside. A few months ago a satellite TV arrived, which provided some distraction in the form of American soap operas in English. Salma wears her hair short like a boy, a rarity in Gaza where the men like women's hair to be long. When she leaves her four square meters to make tea for her father-in-law, Salma wears a little cap. She is strikingly beautiful, and her cap makes her look like a chic young Western woman. It's a style that starkly contrasts with her daily reality. If you ask her if she's happy with Ibrahim, she replies unenthusiastically with a ready-made formula, and no more: "*al-hamdullilah*" (thanks be to God). She has advised her own younger sisters not to marry too young.

While the smallness of the houses pushes the men outside, the women have not built up similar networks of sociability in the Gaza refugee camps. Lack of room prevents them from meeting together out of the men's sight. Nevertheless, not every family is as conservative as Abu Jamal's. Salma's neighbor, for example, fought hard with her husband to win the right to work. A mother of six children, she consigns the smallest to her elder daughters, aged eleven and twelve, who take turns looking after them. One goes to school in the morning, the other in the afternoon. And the second wage the mother now earns is very welcome for feeding and clothing the family, or for decorating their meager home.

The official rules of the UN relief agency originally prohibited the conversion of "shelters" into masonry buildings, but, confronted with the natural growth of the population, the agency made its norms more flexible and adopted a laissez-faire policy. Since the Israeli Army's withdrawal, those of the camp's inhabitants who have the means to do so have improved their conditions. During the first Intifada, the refugees stopped all new construction for fear of Israeli reprisals.[5] But since the coming of Palestinian autonomy, the Gaza camps have been transformed: buildings several stories high have been built to provide lodgings for married sons.

All the same, the recent improvements carried out in Gaza City fed the frustrations of the refugees, who concluded that the Palestinian Authority was neglecting them in favor of the city folk. The reality is that improvements in the camps remain the responsibility of the UN relief agency, which has been steadily proceeding with changes ever since 1996.[6]

BITTERNESS AND OVERCROWDING: THE LIFE OF A REFUGEE

Because the harsh winters required it, refugees in the camps of the West Bank finally rid themselves of their corrugated iron roofs and replaced them with better-insulated terrace ones. The Balata camp, a prolongation of the town of Nablus, is only a few minutes from the urban center. It appears very distinct from its surroundings and remains a place apart despite the improvements made by its inhabitants. The houses are built one against another, thus condemning their inmates to perpetual half-light, if not total darkness. Narrow streets divide the rows of buildings, though asphalt roads have been put through as well to allow vehicles to enter and a market to be held.

The families of Balata all know one another, and some originally came from the same villages. Over the years, forced proximity and the sense of a shared destiny have bound the refugees and their offspring even closer together. Umm Ahmed is one of the foremost figures of the Balata camp. During the first Intifada she did as much as she could during the demonstrations. She would rush out to help the shebab when they were intercepted by Israeli soldiers, clinging and shrieking.

"That's my son and that's my nephew! Let me take them home!"

"What a giant family," the young recruits responded in disbelief.

Umm Ahmed was frequently treated roughly by young Israeli recruits, but still she managed to wrest plenty of local teenagers from their grasp.

Today she looks older than her sixty-four years. She never learned to read and write: when she was ten, she went to see the village *moukhtar* (traditional headman) for help in convincing her parents to send her to school. But the *nakba* (catastrophe) put an end to her ambition to study. Along with her parents and her seven brothers and sisters, she was forced to leave her village near Jaffa. Hers was a peasant family, living off the land; her father decided to head for Salfit, in the Nablus region, where he bought a plot of ground. When they arrived at Salfit, their new life was so precarious that they decided the five boys had to be educated if they were ever to pull through. To survive, four of them chose a second exile abroad. As for Umm Ahmed, she lived for a few years in this new village, until her marriage to a man from her own original home. A young bride of fifteen, she moved to a one-room shelter at Balata supplied by the UNRWA. "I never wanted to get married," she recalls. "I was forced to by my family. We had no money when we arrived at Salfit. When that happens, people have to push out their daughters."

Umm Ahmed's husband started a poultry business. His stall was in the house where they lived. The head of the family killed the chickens and his wife boiled the water, dipped the birds and plucked them. They had twelve children and worked hard to give them an education and a place to live. The first generation of refugees was sometimes illiterate, but it did its best to educate its offspring. Since they had nothing else to bequeath their children, they invested in education. The acquisition of knowledge constituted a kind of moveable capital that people could hang onto whatever their fortunes in life. In spite of their poverty, the camp residents tried to give their children a chance, and the parents' ambitions were evident regarding their choices of study and career.

Umm Ahmed is quite clear that she was never especially happy with her husband. There was never any love between them, and now the best part of her life is behind her: her children, apart from the two youngest, are all married. The boys all went to university. The girls have passed their high school exams. She in her turn obliged two of her daughters to get married. "What was the use of getting more education? They just had to look after their own children. We had no more money to spend on studies, and in any case when the Intifada came all that went by the board. The best thing that could happen was for them to find husbands who could protect them," says the old lady.

Thus history repeats itself. When war brings physical, material, or psychological insecurity to the community, mothers and fathers look to find husbands for their daughters, believing that they will be protected. Furthermore, by ridding itself of female offspring, the family is freed of a double burden: there's one less mouth to feed, and no more need to worry about the girl's virginity. The family's honor remains intact.

Today Umm Ahmed and her husband live in a small, almost cozy three-room apartment with cushions on the sofa. Another floor has been added to their house; one of their sons, married and a father, occupies it. The poultry seller is greatly attached to her little interior and her circumstances: "I love Balata, that I can say. The people here are exiles like we are. I won't ever leave this house. We've worked hard for it and my heart is here. But maybe if they made it possible for us to go back to our village, we'd still go."

Umm Ahmed has returned only once to her birthplace, with her husband's family and her children. Her father's house is still there, lived in by Israelis. The refugees dared not approach it: "I was afraid of them and I know they were afraid of me. There were dogs," she says. The rest of the village has been destroyed.

Umm Ahmed wept when she saw the shattered remains of her childhood. Despite her visceral attachment to the country of her birth, she is ready now to give it up and be content with the West Bank and Gaza. But, she says, "Israel doesn't want peace. Sharon wants to do the same here as he did at Sabra and Chatila." She is pessimistic about the future. For her and her people, she believes, it will just be "more fear, and more bullets."

As a refugee, she has also suffered much at the hands of the towns-people of Nablus. Encouraged by the propaganda of the Arab countries and terrified by the methods of some of the Israeli soldiery, the Pales-tinians of the villages fled before the advancing IDF in 1948. Their re-ception in the towns of the West Bank and the Gaza Strip was far from enthusiastic. The local bourgeoisie paid them rock bottom wages to do menial tasks. In Gaza they were consigned to agricultural labor; in Nablus, they ended up in factories. The women went out to work as housemaids and cleaners for wealthy families. There is still deep resent-ment in Balata for all this. Umm Ahmed says she does not know any Nablusis. "They don't like us. They don't like the refugees. When we ar-rived they treated us like cattle, they insulted us. When we went to get water, they threw dirt in it."

Although she is a good-humored, energetic woman, she looks back on her life with bitterness. Her husband is sick, and she is exhausted. Her legs hurt. She thinks of the miles she walked to visit her sons in prison, the miles she walked to attend the funerals of "martyrs," the back-breaking work she had to do. She criticizes the ineffectual Pales-tinian Authority, which has failed to provide jobs for young people and lets its people die. She thinks the government should pay her some kind of pension for the trouble she has endured on its behalf. "I fought, I re-sisted, I was even hit by rubber bullets," she says. She is critical of the passivity of the Arab states, and she thinks the international community ought to do more to help.

Umm Ahmed's expectations of the Palestinian Authority and for-eign nations reflect her sense of impotence. Ever since going into exile with her family, she has felt that she had no control over her own life. Under such conditions, how could anyone think they had the slightest influence over the destiny of an entire people? Her last act in defiance of her destiny was when she went to the *moukhtar* all those years ago, de-manding to go to school. But ever since the *nakba* put an end to all her projects, Umm Ahmed's existence has been tied to the fate of her nation and the chain of events set off by the upheavals of 1948. Married against her will, she followed her husband to the Balata camp, helped him in his work, and brought twelve children into the world. Even though she did what she could during the first Intifada, she feels that political decisions are all taken in spheres that are totally beyond her. Thus, whenever she ponders the idea of returning home, she expresses not so much a personal longing as an acceptance of political decisions made in high places. In the same way, she counts on being taken care of by the Palestinian Authority—or by foreign donor states.

POLITICAL MOBILIZATION OF THE REFUGEES

With the generation born in the 1960s, this kind of resignation in the face of political and personal destiny gave way to outright revolt. In the late 1970s, Hussam Khader was one of the angry young men who tackled the task of mobilizing Palestinian society.[7]

At that time the camp was in the vanguard of resistance to the occupation. Through the Shabiba action committee, Fatah controlled the camp, recruiting young men to take part in sporting and cultural events and work for the common weal. The shebab punished or drove out collaborators along with people of immoral conduct and then managed to evict the Israeli Army as well. In the early 1980s, the IDF would only venture into the alleyways of Balata when their curfew was in force. A month before the start of the uprising, the civil administration launched a wide-ranging operation aimed at breaking the model of liberation that Balata had become. The soldiers managed to arrest a certain number of suspects but came up short against the camp's residents, fully mobilized and determined to thwart their intrusion.[8] The camps in the West Bank and Gaza provided the bulk of the leaders and manpower of the uprising. The strength of their social ties made it possible for them to structure groups of militants that were both effective and concerted. The sense of unity felt by Balata's people made it much easier for them to defend their camp against the Israelis. In addition, its opaque structure provided perfect shelter for the activists it had nurtured. With its dark alleys and adjoining houses, the camp was an impassable labyrinth to anyone who did not live there.

Today, the camp residents have to defend themselves from the incursions of the Palestinian security forces. Even though many of the people in it support Fatah and themselves work for the Palestinian

Authority, they present a united front against attempts to use force against them. Just as the refugees set about squeezing out the Israelis, they now refuse the Palestinian police admittance to a territory over which they are a law unto themselves. When Najy was threatened with arrest during the al-Aqsa Intifada, he bragged that the Palestinian Authority would never get into Balata to find him.

The overwhelming participation of the refugees in the Intifada had the effect of modifying the way they were perceived. The camp residents, who were habitually placed at the very bottom of the social ladder, had won themselves the status of heroic combatants. The second and third generations of refugees, both in Gaza and in the West Bank, proclaimed their pride in belonging to the camp. This change had a triumphant effect even on the oldest inhabitants. Umm Ahmed described the disdainful reaction of the Nablusis when the refugees first appeared in 1948, but she also stated her view that "today, we're just as good as they are."

Nevertheless, the younger contingent in Chati and Balata have different ambitions. While some wish to continue living in the camp, others hope to move to town one day, even though they haven't the means. This divergence is to be compared with the relationships between the refugees and the dominant society. The conflictual character of the relations between Balata and Nablus and the rancor felt by the camp residents toward the townspeople seem to have fed a desire in the former to raise their social status. To move to town was to prove that you could live just as well as the "Nablusi bourgeois." Najy admits he spends most of his time in Balata, because of his friends and because his role as a fighter takes him back there all the time, but all the same he derives a certain satisfaction from the fact that his house is in a residential area of Nablus. "I wouldn't go back to live in the camp," he says. "Once you've made progress, there's no looking back. And my daughters get sick when I take them down there."

In Gaza, while social differences between townspeople and refugees are still very strong, the actual tensions between the two sides are less so. Townspeople outnumber refugees; moreover, the traditional elites' position is not nearly so firmly entrenched as it is in Nablus, especially since the coming of Palestinian autonomy. While the Chati residents tend to view the Gaza people as unsociable, lacking in solidarity, and not very patriotic, they express no real hostility toward them.

Hussam Khader, a Populist MP

Even though he had been struck off the official Fatah list by the leadership, Hussam Khader decided to stand in the 1996 election in the Territories. The fact that he won his seat as a member of Parliament showed that he had solid local support. It also constituted a resounding personal victory for a domestic militant over Yasser Arafat.

Hussam Khader stands for certain ethical and political principles, and to some extent he regrets the system of national and social revolution that he actively helped to install in the early 1980s. According to him, the battle against Israel called for a complete reorganization of society. Harmful elements had to be jettisoned and a sense of mutual assistance fostered, along with civic pride, cohesion, and a knowledge and love of the motherland. Today the MP feels that these qualities are being supplanted by the individualism arising from a corrupt political system. With a few close associates, he has founded a cultural center for the adolescents in the camp. The principle by which it operates is similar to the one put in place at the time of the Shabiba. By providing cultural and sporting activities, the center's aim is to give the young an understanding of politics and to inculcate certain essential moral values. The behavior of the "friends of the Jaffa cultural center" must be impeccable, on pain of expulsion. In this way the MP has managed to carry on his mission to educate the people, which he began twenty years ago.

Hussam Khader demands as much from himself as he does from others, but as a character he is far from austere. In fact he is lighthearted, optimistic, and sociable. A man of conviction, he speaks directly and does not hesitate to enter the political lists. His battle with Ghassan Shaka, the mayor of Nablus, has politicized and exacerbated the social conflict between the Nablus bourgeoisie and the Balata camp refugees.

When Ghassan Shaka was nominated for mayor in 1994, the residents of Balata noted a sudden sharp rise in their electricity and water bills. They took their complaints to Hussam Khader. To pay off debts accumulated during the Intifada,[9] the Nablus municipality appears to have practically doubled its rates. "Shaka's selling water and electricity for the highest rates in the region. In Gaza, a kilowatt costs 34 agurat (about 10 U.S. cents), and in Nablus the price is 85 agurat (about

25 cents)," explains Hussam Khader. Demonstrations were organized in front of city hall, and the MP raised the matter before the Legislative Council and the Parliamentary Economic Committee. A committee of inquiry was created, but according to Khader it never got off the ground. So he advised the Balata camp residents to stop paying the utility bills sent by the municipality and did likewise himself, in both his home and his office. His justification for this rebellion against local institutions is a simple one. "Shaka is asking for money from people who have nothing and no jobs. In Nablus, 3,200 households have to do without electricity and several hundred lack water, because Shaka doesn't care about other people's hardships."

Hussam Khader is sorry for the poor people of Nablus who cannot defend themselves against the oppression of men like Shaka. But in Balata the situation is entirely different. Even though the majority of people there don't pay, the camp remains connected to the utilities network. The mayor, powerful though he is, dares not deprive Balata of basic services. The consequence would be a general revolt. Khader, himself the son of a refugee, confirms this: "We're fiercely independent people. Nobody pushes Balata around. We're ready to defend ourselves against tyranny." He notes ironically that under the increasingly tense circumstances, the mayor has recruited even more bodyguards.

Hussam Khader knows Sami, Najy, and Bassam very well; indeed, he considers himself a bit like their older brother. Obviously, as a politician he disapproves of their impulsive and chaotic ways, and occasionally he tries to make them see reason. However, in any dispute between shebab and the central authorities or city hall, he remains unconditionally on his own people's side. Even though some of his ties can be awkward, it is doubtless in the interest of the MP to maintain this solidarity and to be able to count on the support of a few armed shebab should he ever need them. Khader has never been a supporter of violence as a mean to an end. Nevertheless, the brutal turns that political quarrels in Palestine sometimes take oblige him to be on his guard.

Hussam Khader's base in Balata does not stop him from having broader ambitions. He now heads the Committee for the Defense of the Rights of Refugees, which has branches throughout the territory. As a long-time domestic militant for Fatah, he has come up against one of the strongest elements in the makeup of Palestinian society—its parochialism. Political loyalties and political identities are invariably forged at the local level. Apart from Yasser Arafat, there are very few people in the Territories who can claim truly national stature.

The Palestinian Legislative Council

Members of the Palestinian Legislative Council have genuine popular legitimacy. The legislative and presidential elections of January 1996 came off in a generally satisfactory way, even though there were a few minor irregularities. Some 79.7 percent of the electorate cast a vote, a clear indication of society's will to take part and eagerness to set up a system of national representation. Yet the electoral campaign and the balloting did not exactly create the conditions for real political competition. For example, the Islamist and Marxist oppositions boycotted the election because of their opposition to the Oslo accords, holding themselves aloof from the new political structure. The battle for seats in the assembly involved mostly Fatah candidates, even though the majority stood as independents. Furthermore, the elections were somewhat short on political debate, the candidates preferring to dwell on the themes of national unity and the process of national liberation. Worse, the division of the Territories into very small constituencies tended to favor the dynamic of personal ties over ideological preference.

The voters returned a majority of Yasser Arafat's political party. It was a landslide for Fatah, and it raised fears of a rubber stamp assembly for the leader's executive decisions. As it turned out, the Legislative Council was impelled by its complement of domestic Palestinian figures to affirm a broad measure of independence. It showed pluck when it tackled the burning issue of corruption, creating a committee of inquiry in 1997 that directly implicated several members of the government by accusing them of bad management and diversion of funds. These criticisms brought about the collective resignation of Arafat's entire cabinet of ministers. Yet although the corruption affair dominated the council's deliberations for over a year, the MPs later renounced their own action by an overwhelming vote of confidence in the very same government when it was proposed a second time by the head of the Palestinian Authority. Outraged by the political cowardice of the MPs, Hussam Khader made a remark that raised hackles: "While we're at it, why don't we vote a law affirming that Yasser Arafat is God? After all, he can transform generals into foot soldiers and foot soldiers into generals. Also he can make poor men rich and rich men poor." This provoked some angry reactions; one MP tried to assault his colleague and had to be restrained. "Don't worry," Khader sneered, "you're sure to get a house and a car from Yasser Arafat, for being such a loyal fellow."

Yasser Arafat managed to short-circuit the vague desires of the political class by rallying the majority of MPs to his own system of power. What exactly was negotiated between the Old Man and the council members has yet to emerge, though one imagines that the promise of political appointments and funds for personal activities or projects won over quite a few of them. These maneuvers by the president of the Authority were part of a strategy to sideline the parliament, whose debates now ceased to be broadcast by the Palestinian TV channel. The executive power largely ignored what the council did; Arafat would not always agree to sign the laws voted by the legislature, nor even to apply those that he had signed. For example, he refused to condone the fundamental legal code proposed by the parliament. In the absence of a constitution to set the prerogatives of the executive, legislative, and judiciary powers and define the relationship among them, legislators had no legal framework within which they could oppose the president. Arafat didn't bother with the law; his legitimacy, as he well knew, was personal and revolutionary, and he used it to extend the PLO's function as an organization of national liberation. While there was no Palestinian state, it was out of place to demand a regular state's rule of law.

More often than not, Yasser Arafat's methods overruled the wishes of those who were looking for democracy and real change. An attempt by the MP Azmi al-Shuaybi to make the executive adopt rules of financial probity and openness ended in failure. As a minister in the first government of the Palestinian Authority in 1998, Azmi al-Shuaybi led the budget committee in an attempt to force Yasser Arafat to account for the revenues and outgoings of the treasury and present a formal budget to the Palestinian Legislative Council. His investigations uncovered a number of irregularities, notably the fact that some of the expenses set out in the budget were completely fictional, and that 126 million dollars of public money had been placed in various foreign accounts. When al-Shuaybi was about to reveal his findings to the council, intense pressure from Arafat on the other members of the committee forced him to resign his post and stop his work. The former minister, in his analysis of the democratic shortcomings of the Palestinian Authority, makes it clear that the Authority's financial irregularities are largely due to the fact that it has to rely on a "strategic reserve fund." Since it depends on the tax and customs revenue that Israel periodically pays over, it is vulnerable to a suspension of these payments in the event of a political disagreement with the Israelis. In making sure he has permanent access to hard cash, Yasser Arafat is merely taking out insurance against an uncertain future. He also uses the funds to reward his close associates, as well as people who refrain from openly opposing him. In short, Arafat's grip on the Authority's finances gives him the means to assert effective control over its political life and institutions.[10]

Thus the Palestinian president maintains a docile cabinet, insofar as he has personal control over the way funds are apportioned to each ministry. Moreover, he deals with each minister in a directly personal way that gives him formidable power. According to Azmi al-Shuaybi, appointments within the administration directly sanction the functionaries' political allegiance to Yasser Arafat.[11] By working directly with individuals, the head of the Palestinian Authority dilutes its institutions and fosters confusion between the public and private spheres. Thus the Council of Ministers has been suspended, which means there is no give-and-take whatever among the different members of the government; ministers are obliged to deal exclusively with the president. By placing his subordinates in positions of rivalry, the leader strengthens his own central position, the power of his functionaries deriving not from their status or their job, but from their relative closeness to Yasser Arafat.

Thus political life within the Authority is kept firmly under control. Fatah itself is unable to shake off its leader's controlling hand, or to impose itself as a genuine force in Palestinian politics. Its representatives too are hampered by their political and economic dependence on Arafat's system of power. The movement's finances are entirely directed by the leader's choices. The distribution of positions within the administration or the party, as well as of material advantages, ensures the loyalty of individuals. Few members of Fatah have the personal resources or the personal legitimacy to break away from the *rais* and survive in politics thereafter.

This situation affects the legitimacy of the political class. The population resents the powerlessness of their elected representatives to affect the national destiny. Some feel that the MPs "do nothing for the people" and rail against the privileges they accumulate, such as their high salaries and cars with red number plates (meaning they belong to the Authority), which give them freedom of movement both within the Territories and in Israel. Since the start of the al-Aqsa Intifada, the MPs on the Legislative Council have lost this right, and the total blockade of the West Bank and the Gaza Strip now prevents the parliament from meeting at Ramallah. It tried to overcome this by using a videoconference system, but this idea did not work at all and was soon abandoned.

The MPs' inability to fulfill their legislative role and their representative function does not necessarily make them entirely useless. They are much in demand by their constituents. In a society that is still deeply marked by tradition, it is habitual for people to look for a mediator to settle personal difficulties. All too often the defective institutional and administrative system of Palestinian autonomy fails to satisfy the people's demands. Going to a government representative to apply for a job or a loan, to deal with a dispute with a neighbor, or to help in a disagreement with the security services is common practice. The fact that people deplore the nepotism and management methods used by the Authority is neither here nor there. They resort to exactly the same procedures when they need to resolve a difficulty or improve their personal situation.

The aptitude of MPs to respond to these many demands depends above all on their connections. Those who are integrated into the system and who are on good terms with the decision-making centers have all the resources they need to maintain networks of loyalties. The others can perform the same services for their constituents only by using their own financial resources. Dr. Muaiya al-Masri belongs to one of the more powerful Nablusi families, though he comes from its less wealthy branch. During the election campaign, he found himself competing against his cousin, Maher al-Masri, who was the Fatah candidate and Yasser Arafat's nominee for minister of economy. Both men came out winners. The doctor's candidacy was frequently presented as that of a man close to the Islamist movement. His activities as a manager and distributor within the town's *zakat* committee, along with his personal religious commitment, gave force to this reputation. For his own part, Muaiya al-Masri campaigned as an independent unconnected to any party. He believes the electors chose him because of his readiness to help the needy. Having earned plenty of money during his years of work in Saudi Arabia and Kuwait, he had come back to exercise his profession in Nablus. "I've never asked my patients to pay me one penny," says the old doctor. "And often enough I've supplied their medicine free of charge." Today he has an office in the center of town where he receives visitors from dawn to dusk. His waiting room is always full, and the doctor considers it his duty to listen to and help each person if he can. "Anyone who comes to see me here, whether I know him or not, goes away with a solution to his problem." For his own support, this particular MP can rely on revenue derived from his shares in his family's business. A man comes to tell him his brother has been wrongly arrested by the police. Muaiya al-Masri writes a letter and obtains his release. A family complains that it is unable to pay its medical insurance bill to the Authority; the doctor pays two-thirds of the 1,000 shekels required (about U.S. $300). A sterile women tells him she can't afford an operation, and he calls a fellow doctor to ask him to lower the price by 50 percent. When people whose houses have been destroyed by the Israelis apply to him, he sends them on to the regional governor. With the new Intifada and the social and economic crisis it has engendered, requests like these are more and more frequent, and the queue of people waiting to see Dr. al-Masri grows ever longer.

Dr. al-Masri's interventions are inspired by a long local and family tradition. The patrician class of Nablus, with their charitable associations, bring relief to the poor while maintaining bonds of dependency that shore up their position. This system of patronage uses resources and networks that differ from those of the Palestinian Authority.

MPs who belong to the opposition and who can count on only the record of a respected family or a personal fortune are not so well placed to satisfy their electors' needs. Yet to remain popular they have to play the game. While he distances himself from Yasser Arafat's inner circle and roundly condemns corruption in the government, Hussam Khader, through his history as a militant and Fatah operative, continues to use certain contacts. When confronted with people needing jobs, he makes telephone calls to smooth their way to a place in a government department or one of the security services. In spite of himself, with actions like this he comforts the system he so strongly criticizes. If he serves as an intermediary to promote the recruitment of somebody close to him or someone he knows, in doing so he condones the practice of nepotism. At the same time, he adds to one of the worst characteristics of the Palestinian Authority, which, by creating a huge military bureaucracy, has placed its employees in a posture of moral and financial dependency.

Rafat al-Najar belongs to the Popular Front for the Liberation of Palestine. Born in 1945, he took part in the guerrilla movement against Israel in the early 1970s. After that he spent seventeen years in prison, before being liberated after the Oslo accords. A member of a prominent family from Khan Younes, the southernmost town on the Gaza Strip, Rafat al-Najar decided not to go along with the election boycott announced by his movement. His reasoning was that his engagement on behalf of his nation overruled his engagement as a party activist. In his role as an elected MP, al-Najar joined in the political battle against corruption. Even though he belongs to the opposition, he too finds himself solicited for help by his constituents. He does what he can for them, but he refuses to put pressure on the judicial system on their behalf if they have got themselves in trouble. He is quite clear that services rendered to electors foment rivalry among the MPs. "Everyone tries as hard as they can to resolve people's problems as quickly and effectively as possible. But when we can't, we pass the petitioners on to our colleagues." The help he procures for people in his roundabout way scarcely corresponds to his notion of the role of a representative of the Palestinian nation. Nevertheless, he cannot duck relationships of this kind as long as the population is unable to resign itself to the rational and legal operation of the administration.

LIMITED FREE SPEECH, UNLIMITED VERBIAGE

The Palestinian security forces watch carefully over the political order established in the Territories. They make it clear to the impetuous that overstepping the mark carries a certain risk. The intelligence services, overstaffed as they are, keep a close eye on the population, and what they do sometimes reveals an original notion of the role of security. For example, in June 1996, a Palestinian photographer working for Agence France Presse was arrested and beaten for having published a picture of children playing with a donkey on the beach in Gaza. The pretext for this was that he had spread an unworthy image of Palestine.

Employees and executives of businesses may find themselves summoned for interrogations, during which they are made to divulge information about their work. Such information is hardly of strategic importance and could sometimes be obtained in a simpler way.

Representatives of human rights associations are also frequent targets of the security forces. They have condemned the treatment of illegally detained Islamists, some of whom have been sentenced by unofficial tribunals. They have also challenged the methods of the police by drawing attention to the ill-treatment and torture of prisoners. Some of these human rights representatives found themselves detained for hours, even days at a time. In their euphemistic way, the Palestinian officers speak of "an invitation to drink coffee," which is notoriously served to people detained in the offices of the Preventive Security or General Intelligence Services. Human rights advocates are usually treated with a certain consideration, because of their local reputation and the support they can muster abroad. Nevertheless it is possible to bring pressure to bear on them, to bully them into toning down their criticism of the leadership. After a compulsory visit to the security services, people are liable to moderate their speech or writing, and even to retract some of the things they may have said.

Others are treated much more harshly. Abdelsattar Qassem, a history professor at al-Najah University, made a number of caustic statements about the Palestinian leadership. In 1995 he was shot and wounded in the leg by masked assailants. In late 1999 he was jailed for putting his name to a petition, "The Appeal of the Twenty," a virulent attack on the government. Its authors established a link between corruption among Palestine's leaders and political concessions made to Israel. "The Palestinian Authority is conducting a formidable policy of corruption, humiliation, and exploitation of the Palestinian people, as if the Oslo accords gave them license to use the motherland like a private business for the enrichment of a few." The document was an implicit incitement to rebellion: "Let us make a stand together against this tyranny and corruption. Injustice can only be crushed by a concerted action of the disinherited."

The events that followed illustrate the Authority's ambiguous way of dealing with opposition. Some of the signatories to the tract were beaten or detained by the intelligence services. Some got off relatively lightly, because of the parliamentary immunity that the Legislative Council refused to withdraw, despite pressure from the executive. Hussam Khader was contacted by the security apparatus and agreed to distance himself publicly from the "Appeal of the Twenty." All the same, he supported some of their views of corruption. Abdeljawad Saleh, the mayor of al-Bireh who had been deposed and driven out by the Israelis in 1970, was a respected figure; an MP with a huge majority in Ramallah, he was on the side of the petitioners. In the course of an inquiry about the fate of those of the "Twenty" who had been forced into hiding, he was severely beaten at the headquarters of the Preventive Security force. This incident was presented as an error by overzealous officers acting on their own initiative. In fact it demonstrated the astonishingly free hand given to the security apparatus, as well as the repressive nature of the new political order. This tendency fed on the ambition of political and administrative leaders whose priorities were to forestall dissent and preserve their own power. The MPs were aware of the influence wielded by the security forces and knew that their attitude would decide who succeeded Yasser Arafat. Nevertheless, some of them were not fully resigned to this and dared to speak out. As militants in the 1970s and 1980s and veterans of the struggle against Israeli repression, they refused to bend to the Authority's will.

Despite the presence of students employed by the security services, the Palestinian universities remained a forum for political discussion. While some of the current student leaders had spent time in prison, new elections to student councils were held every year. The Islamist sweep in most of the faculties of the West Bank and the Gaza Strip shows that these ballots were freely organized and that the Palestinian Authority had not succeeded in controlling every aspect of political life.

In 1996 the Palestinian police entered the campus of al-Najah University in Nablus, arrested about a hundred students, and closed down the faculty for a week. This caused outrage and fury throughout the

West Bank. Yasser Arafat tried to calm things down by declaring that the students would be freed. The president of the Court of Justice ruled that there was no case for them to answer and they must be released. His decision was not carried out. A delegation of twelve MPs led by the president of the parliament, Abu Ala, asked for an audience with the *rais*. Rafat al-Najar was one of them. Abu Ala confronted Arafat, he recalls. He said: "We've learned from you that no one is above the law. A legal decision has been made. So why don't the security services release the students?" Arafat replied: "Of course nobody's above the law. But the judge ought to have asked me before he made his decision. Otherwise, why on earth am I the president?" The MPs gaped. Abu Ala tried to prolong the interview, but to no avail.

On another level, contacts and speaking out can have an effect on the way decisions go. Hussam Khader will intervene whenever he is convinced that somebody has been made a victim of an abuse of power. For example, he went to police headquarters when one of his Balata friends was thrown in jail after a dispute with a neighbor. Similarly, he opposed the arrest of the camp shebab when they were accused of illegally possessing weapons. He succeeded in convincing the chief of police to change his mind, thus averting a confrontation between his men and the young men of the camp. Resorting to methods like these is not much of a guarantee of democracy, but it does create some kind of counterbalance to the power of the central government. No attempt to intercede is sure of success, since it depends on the degree of personal contact the petitioner has with the Authority, as well as his ability to negotiate and convince.

The politicians show a certain disposition to dialogue, negotiation, and dealing. Their debates, which usually take place in private, supply some sort of basis for a system of consultation, and this mitigates the authoritarian nature of the regime. All manner of problems can lead to the calling of a meeting between political and military officials. While the results of these discussions are seldom satisfactory to the defenders of liberty, they show that there is a willingness to find solutions to conflicts under certain circumstances. At the same time, they demonstrate not only the government's consummate skill at controlling the political arena, but also the unavoidable fact that autonomous Palestine bears no resemblance at all to a democratic regime. In any case, the loud objections voiced by some of the parties are preventing the government from totally annexing Palestinian political life.

The Islamists, who remain outside the national representative system and are trying to make a mark on the regional scene by the use of violence, continue to feed the repressive nature of the regime.[12] Under pressure from Israel and the international community, the Palestinian Authority is attempting to neutralize the structures of Hamas and Islamic Jihad. The resumption of hostilities between Israel and the Palestinians has greatly weakened the case for arresting Islamists. The supporters of the Oslo accords could accept that those responsible for sending out suicide bombers should be jailed. They could also tolerate or at least turn a blind eye to the conditions of their detention, as long as members of Hamas and Islamic Jihad obstructed negotiations with Israel. But now that the peace process appears to have come to a complete standstill and the Israeli Army is back with a vengeance, society feels that it is fundamentally wrong to keep on punishing the Islamists.

Yet in spite of the deepening rift within the Territories, the threatened Palestinian civil war has not come about. There have been a number of clashes between the Islamist militants and the police, but until now Hamas and Islamic Jihad have shown restraint in not attacking the representatives of the regime.

Nevertheless, the hunting down of the militants and heads of the Islamist tendency has come to be the principal obstacle to the rule of law in Palestine. A resolution of the Palestinian question and the lowering of tensions are indispensable if the political system is ever to become truly democratic. The more encroachments on Palestinian sovereignty that Israel makes to safeguard its own security, the greater the toll on the nature and construction of the Palestinian entity, which bears the scars of its military, political, and economic dependence.

CHAPTER FOUR

Palestine and Israel: The Impossible Divorce

No study of Palestinian society and institutions can avoid an analysis of the relationship with Israel. The coming of the autonomous regime in the Gaza Strip and in part of the West Bank has brought a change in the way Israel maintains its grip on the Palestinians, rather than a loosening of that grip or its disappearance altogether.

The rising anguish of the Israelis as attacks on them grew more and more frequent led their leaders to devise a system of security that was supposed to neutralize the Palestinian danger once and for all. The occupation years had been marked by Israel's will to integrate the Territories economically, and thus demonstrate the nonviability of an independent Palestinian state. By contrast, the present system shows a will to bring about a physical separation, a clean break. The elites of the Israeli state were counting on a hermetically sealed frontier between the two entities to ensure the tranquility of their fellow citizens; at the same time they meant to extricate themselves from the occupation, which had turned into an intolerable moral, political, and military burden. Nevertheless, the Israeli leaders tried to create conditions favorable to economic development in the Territories, taking the view that an improvement in Palestinian living standards would ultimately yield political peace. But economic encouragement would always be subordinate to the immediate imperative of protecting Israel.

In effect, Israel set out to renew its relationship with the Palestinians by reverting to the idea of a separation of the two societies.

The project came up against the intricacies of spaces and people. Those making the decisions had to use their imaginations as well as technology to get around the myriad geographical and economic restraints. Meanwhile, the Palestinian Authority, which did not have the means to obstruct the Israeli project, made an effort to negotiate the best possible deal.

Thus the Israeli state imposed ever tighter controls on the movement of people and goods out of the West Bank and the Gaza Strip. The proliferation and the slowness of their inspection procedures became a serious drag on Palestinian economic development. Moreover, the sophistication of the Israeli apparatus for differentiating between various categories of Palestinians created widening socioeconomic fissures and made the fragmentation of the Palestinian Territories even worse.

PALESTINIAN WORKERS IN ISRAEL

From the earliest years of the occupation, Israel encouraged its business sector to lure Palestinians to work in Israeli territory. This policy sealed Palestinian economic dependence on Israel, but it also contributed to raising living standards among the inhabitants of the West Bank and Gaza. The Palestinians may have represented cheap labor for Israeli entrepreneurs, but still the wages earned were higher than they would have been in the Territories. Indeed, the average income per capita in the Territories doubled between 1972 and 1992.

Between 1970 and 1980, the majority of working-class Palestinian families sent at least one male across to work in Israel, and during school holidays teenage boys would go to work alongside their father to round out the family income. This sector of the population learned to speak Hebrew and maintained personal contacts with Israeli society. There were often very good relationships between the Palestinian workers and their Israeli colleagues or bosses. As a rule the former avoided discussing political topics or disagreeing with their superiors. They had to, because the renewal of their contracts or their permits depended on their Israeli employers. Men with families were reluctant to risk their jobs for their convictions.

To avoid being in an inferior position, some Palestinians concealed their identity and masqueraded as Israelis. Fuad, one of the Nablus shebab, worked as a house-mover in Israel. "I told them I was an Israeli," he recalls. "My brother did too. He became an Israeli from top to toe—you'd never know he was an Arab. He spoke perfect Hebrew. He told them he'd been in the army and he'd killed five Arabs. They all congratulated him." To fool the enemy, to mimic his most extreme ideas, to adopt his outward demeanor—all these were ways of turning the tables, or at least of convincing oneself that one had escaped the reality of the situation. In any event, the sense of duping one's foe gave a certain satisfaction, even at the risk of losing one's own identity.

Ghassan lived in the Jabalya camp in the Gaza strip. A trained teacher, he decided to go to work in Israel because the wages were higher. The extra money would make it possible for him to marry. Through a cousin who was already there, he found work as a butcher in a suburban Ashquelon supermarket. His boss provided lodgings, a small apartment that he shared with three other Palestinians from Gaza. They lived and ate together, with no women and no family anywhere near. The naked pinups on the walls bore witness to their sudden freedom. Ghassan assumed a new first name, with the full knowledge and encouragement of his Israeli co-workers. It was a typically Jewish name "so the customers wouldn't be alarmed," he says. He was ready to adopt the attitude of the beaten man, who would forsake his identity as an Arab and internalize the stigma of posing a danger to the master. In doing so he fitted himself exactly to the standard Israeli's negative view of his people.

Yet the dismal economic state of the Gaza Strip obliged its people to seek work on the other side of the Green Line. Up to 1993, the Israeli job market absorbed between 35 and 40 percent of the workforce in Gaza, and between 25 and 30 per cent of that of the West Bank. After Oslo, these proportions fell respectively to 15 percent and 20 percent.[1] Even though 167,000 jobs were created in the West Bank and Gaza Strip between 1995 and 2000, this progress did not add up to a significant reduction in Palestinian dependence on Israel. Nor did it bring an end to unemployment.[2] When the Israeli authorities closed off the Territories, the number of jobless more than doubled, soaring to 32.5 percent in Gaza and 23.8 percent in the West Bank.[3] Today, working in

Israel still has a financial attraction for Palestinians. An ordinary police officer employed by the Palestinian Authority earns about $270 a month, while a worker in Israel can make between $15 and $40 per day—the equivalent of a salary of $360 to $960 for a full month's labor.

Before 1988 the Palestinians could move freely in and out of Israel to find work. After that year, the flux of workers was controlled. In 1991 the Jewish state set up a permit system to regulate Palestinian comings and goings on its territory. Work permits had to be approved by the security services and required a promise of a job from an Israeli employer. The authorization, specifying the name and location of the employer, had to be renewed every two months.[4] Candidates had to be married and over age 28 because the Israeli arbiters considered that young bachelors were more liable to commit acts of violence.

The Israeli economy was profiting from a flexible and cheap workforce based in the Territories. The construction, textile, and agricultural sectors absorbed the majority of Palestinian workers. In the early 1990s, however, Israeli security needs came into conflict with the needs of employers. The administration had set up mechanisms to restrict Palestinian movement in and out of Israel. The number of Palestinian workers with jobs in Israel had fallen, and the vacuum was filled by a labor force from Romania and Southeast Asia.

However, despite its stated wish to contain the Palestinians on the far side of the Green Line, Israel continued to employ them. There were two reasons for this. First, some Israeli entrepreneurs continued to show a preference for Palestinians. Second, the Israeli government felt that employing part of the Palestinian workforce helped to alleviate political tensions between the two sides. Israeli leaders felt that any decline in Palestinian living standards was bound to nourish political extremism and violence. Ever since the coming of the Palestinian Authority and the start of the suicide bombing campaign in Israel, Israeli policy in regard to Palestinian labor had fluctuated wildly. Although there was a patent desire to exclude Palestinian workers, their presence was not totally rejected.

Between 1990 and 1993, Israel employed between 100,000 and 120,000 Palestinians and only a very small number of foreigners. In 1993, reacting to Palestinian attacks, the Labor government reduced the number of people allowed in from the Territories. This tendency was confirmed in 1994, when 60,000 workers from other countries were brought in to Israel. By 1996 this number had risen to 110,000, while the Palestinians now occupied only 30,000 jobs.

All the same, Israel quickly realized the downside to importing new, non-Jewish immigrant workers. First, they brought along with them large numbers of illegal workers. Out of 200,000 to 300,000 foreigners now in Israel, half are illegals. By comparison, Palestinians presented a number of advantages. First of all, they spoke Hebrew and were familiar with the environment. Second, they were trustworthy and effective workers, and in general their employers were satisfied with them. Third, and above all, unlike the Romanians and Southeast Asians, they went home in the evening. Bringing in non-Jewish foreigners raised the question of their relationship with the host society. The Israelis had to decide whether to integrate, or leave at the margins of society, several new groups that couldn't care less about the political and religious concerns of the Jewish state.

Israeli employers were able to put pressure on the Israeli authorities to admit cheap, trustworthy, and convenient Palestinian workers. Low salaries and the absence of wage claims held out the possibility of extra regulation in the industrial sector, part of which was in decline. The restriction on the Palestinian workers' movements, even a total ban on them, was a real handicap to Israeli employers. The construction industry in particular needed substantial human resources. Between 1993 and 2000, forty-nine new Jewish settlements had appeared on the West Bank, and the number of settlers had doubled. Houses and new bypass roads for the settlers to skirt Palestinian areas had to be built. The construction sector grew by 8.7 percent per year during this period, and the existing Israeli and foreign workforce was insufficient to meet the demand. In 1998 Palestinian workers still represented 25 percent of the men on Israeli building sites.[5] The election of Benyamin Netanyahu in May 1996 had marked a turning point in Israeli policy concerning foreign workers in Israel. A general uneasiness caused by the presence of the immigrants combined with the ideological stance of the Likud had brought about the change.[6] The nationalist right was opposed to the idea of a separation between Israel and the Territories. In effect, the application of this idea presupposed the eventual formation of a sovereign Palestinian state. Thus, from the end of 1997 onward, the number of

Palestinians allowed to seek work in Israel increased, and by December some 48,000 extra permits had been granted in the West Bank and Gaza.[7] In 1998 the rightist Israeli government adopted several measures aimed at clearing the way for Palestinian workers. The age limit to apply for a permit was lowered to twenty-three.[8] A certain category of workers was allowed to stay overnight close to their workplace in Israel. At the same time, the Netanyahu government set about repatriating an average of five hundred illegal immigrants from other countries every month, and punishing Israeli firms that employed them.

Ehud Barak's government, which came to power in 1999, did not tamper with the Palestinian employment policy. In 2000, before the start of the Intifada, 115,000 West Bank people were earning a living in Israel (half of them illegally), and 30,000 Gazans had official Israeli work permits. But the new wave of violence that began in September 2000 changed the situation again, when the territory was sealed off and all work permits suspended. Nevertheless, about 20,000 West Bankers continued to cross the line illegally and sell their work to Israeli entrepreneurs, while the settlements and the industrial zones[9] still employed several thousand Palestinians.

ISRAELI SECURITY, PALESTINIAN CONTAINMENT

In the early 1990s, Israel set up a permit system to regulate the movements of Palestinian migrant workers. The freedom of movement of people in and out of Jerusalem and Israel, or between Gaza and the West Bank, was considerably reduced. Work in Israel, attendance at West Bank universities by Gazans, family visits, and medical care all took place at the whim of the Israeli civil administration.[10]

The series of suicide attacks against Israeli civilians that began in 1994 had caused this hardening of attitudes. The loss of freedom of movement directly affected most of the population, and it was paradoxical that at the very moment when the Palestinians were at last achieving some kind of self-government, they were losing the ability to travel where they wished. In terms of daily life, the signing of the peace accords coincided with the beginning of a new containment.

As the negotiations proceeded and the prospect of a Palestinian state drew closer, the Israeli leaders pinned their hopes on perfecting their control mechanisms over the Palestinians. Bureaucratic procedures and different types of status proliferated; several categories of Palestinians were thus created as a function of where they lived, along with their socioeconomic and political circumstances. The sophistication of this mechanism augured well for its durability.

Palestinians of the West Bank and Gaza had to carry a special authorization from the Israeli state to cross the Green Line legally. They could not obtain this precious document if their political past had been classified "security risk" by the Israeli security service. Many of the shebab of the Intifada, as street militants of a political formation, were condemned to total immobility. The ways in which the authorizations were granted corresponded to the work the applicants expected to do. Most salaried workers were forbidden to remain in Israeli territory after 7 p.m. Individuals could obtain exit permits for personal reasons, to visit a relative or undergo surgery, for one or several days. Businesspeople were subjected to less drastic conditions.[11] They were allowed to stay in Israel, and a hundred or so of them who lived in Gaza were allowed to use "sterilized" cars, which were left in locked car lots on the edge of Erez. If these cars were taken back to Gaza, they could not come out again. This meant that those concerned had to have two cars: one for Gaza, the other for Israel. Some had VIP cards, but nearly all of these were distributed to high officials of the Palestinian Authority. Israel also gave special treatment to ministers, deputies, and heads of security services. These people did not need to ask for specific authorization in order to get out of the Territories, and some were even allowed to drive their own Palestine-registered cars to and fro.

GAZA IN CHAINS

The Israeli procedures for controlling traffic with the West Bank and Gaza were very different. Israelis viewed the Gaza Strip as a hotbed of extremists strongly inclined to violence, a place full of dangerous subversives. The Intifada had begun in the Gaza refugee camps, and its people had made a significant contribution to the national Palestinian struggle. They were to be feared, and their portion of Palestine was viewed as a demographic time bomb. In 1994 the birthrate in Gaza was a record 7.4 children for every woman.[12] Furthermore, in the eyes of the Israelis, the working-class people of Gaza were much more radical than the West Bank Palestinians, and based on these conclusions they went out of their way to protect themselves against the Gazans.

Two factors facilitated the isolation of Gaza. To begin with, ultra-nationalist and religious elements among the Israelis have mostly stayed out of Gaza. There are only about five thousand settlers there. Second, the fact that the zone was so small, measuring forty kilometers long and ten kilometers wide, made it a simple matter to deploy specific means there. After the transfer of power to the Palestinian Authority, the Israelis built an electric fence around the territory. The Erez checkpoint, now the only way into Israel, has been rebuilt as a full-fledged frontier post since 1994.

Transiting individuals at Erez are subjected to different procedures and channels, according to their status. Workers employed in Israel and occasional visitors walk across the five hundred-meter no-man's-land, a sort of security cordon between the Palestinian police barrier and the Israel control point. After this they have to go through a separate channel that is fully wired off and covered, to doors behind which they are checked and manually searched by Israeli soldiers.

Foreigners (tourists, UN agency staff) and holders of VIP cards are all treated equally and do not have to pass through with the Palestinian workers. If their car has clearance, they can cross the no-man's-land in it. They then go into an office where their IDs are checked and their bags are put through an X-ray machine. Meanwhile the car is looked over by a trained team supplied by a private security firm. Once all this has been done, the travelers receive a ticket bearing essential information about them (number of passengers, number of bags), which will enable them to carry on through the Israeli checkpoint at the far end of the Erez terminal.

All these procedures were installed in the course of 1998; previously, there were faceoffs in front of the posts, and baggage and vehicle checks were unsystematic. Foreigners and VIPs could avoid them or else found themselves going through endless questioning and searches by the soldiers. The new rules make the whole process much more rational and give it an air of correctness combined with strictness. The soldiers, comfortably installed behind their desks, have been told to be agreeable. The precision of the procedures leaves little room for discussion or negotiation between the Israeli Army and people passing through, which means that wrong moves and abuses are avoided.

Israeli citizens are forbidden to go to Gaza; their own country's authorities refuse them this permission for security reasons. However, special permits can be obtained if the circumstances are exceptional. As for the settlers in the Gaza Strip, they have their own checkpoint, which they reach by roads reserved for their own use. Their security is viewed as a priority, to such a point that since 1995 Palestinians and foreigners have been forbidden to use the road along the seashore because there are several settlements nearby.

The electrified barrier is highly effective. It has made it virtually impossible to escape Gaza, and the result is a sense of imprisonment and suffocation. There are 3,766 people to every square kilometer in the territory.[13] The towns, camps, and houses are hideously overpopulated. To escape the watching eyes of one's family and the pressure of the community at large requires almost superhuman ingenuity. People in Gaza live without windows on the outside. The only crumbs of comfort come from encounters with foreigners passing through—or from the dreams peddled by Israeli TV or the satellite channels. The people speak of Gaza as a "rabbit hutch" or a "life-size jail." Most Gazans under twenty have never known anything other than the place where they were born. A test carried out on children and young people from the ages of ten to twenty-four has shown that three out of four think the map of Gaza is the map of Palestine.[14] This inability to picture the national space is an example of how a generation, and indeed a whole society, trapped in a given territory can have its imagination literally amputated by the experience.

❑❑❑

ISRAEL AND THE WEST BANK: AN IMPOSSIBLE SEPARATION

The inhabitants of the West Bank are not so severely restricted in their movements as their brothers in Gaza. The territory covers 6,600 square kilometers, and the presence of 200,000 Jewish settlers would anyway make it difficult as well as costly to effect a complete physical separation with Israel. Moreover, it would condemn everyone living in the settlements to a virtual confinement, alongside the Palestinians. The main obstacle is of course political: for to specify boundaries would be the same as defining the frontiers between Israel and an eventual Palestinian state. And although the Israelis may have voluntarily renounced sovereignty over the Gaza Strip, the prospect of an entirely Palestinian West Bank remains anathema to a sizable body of Israeli public opinion.

Israeli troops staff a number of blockades on the West Bank perimeter. All cars crossing here must pass through checkpoints. The rate at which vehicles go through, heading toward Jerusalem, varies according to the orders given to the Israeli soldiers and the zeal with which they do their work. Only cars with yellow license plates—Israeli ones—are authorized to go through the barriers. IDF troops carefully check the papers of other vehicles, as well as the authorizations carried by their passengers.

Many journeys are made in communal taxis belonging to residents of East Jerusalem, and the cars are rarely searched. In periods of relative calm, it is very easy for West Bank inhabitants to cross the Green Line without permission: the numerous routes leading across are used by taxi drivers and pedestrians without meeting any challenge from the soldiers. Before the beginning of the al-Aqsa Intifada, and when there were no terrorist attacks going on, the Israeli authorities tolerated these clandestine crossings, which were generally made by illegal workers: between 1997 and 2000, the Israeli Ministry of Defense estimated them at fifty thousand. So the checks imposed on the perimeter of the West Bank simply complicate the daily life of Palestinians, by increasing the time it takes for people to get to work. On the other hand, the checks do not prevent suicide bombers from crossing the Green Line.

In the other direction, from Israel to the West Bank, the IDF soldiers do not interfere with traffic. The only threat they care about is that
of violence by Palestinians on Israeli soil.

BREAKING UP THE TERRITORIES

When the Israeli government considers the threat from the Occupied
Territories to be too great, it activates an internal sealing-off policy that
isolates the Palestinian communities from one another. The IDF is still in
control of 60 percent of the West Bank and 40 percent of the Gaza Strip.
It is easy for the army to erect checkpoints between Palestinian towns
and villages and stop all movement of people and goods. In February
1996, when a dissident branch of Hamas organized a series of terrorist
attacks that killed many people, Israel sealed the territory completely. In
the West Bank the inhabitants and goods carriers could no longer move
further than the outer limits of their town or village. Yet, in a demonstration that the tactic was far from infallible, two more suicide attacks
in March sent the Jewish state into mourning once again.

Today, as a result of the al-Aqsa Intifada, the Israeli authorities have
reverted to the policy of sealing off communities within the Territories.
Two blocks, one in the south and the other in the center of the Gaza
Strip, now divide it into three segments. A journey of some twenty kilometers can take four hours. The West Bank is divided up by a multitude
of checkpoints manned by the IDF; the villages are cut off, and the
army can prevent supplies reaching them for several days at a time.
People who live a few kilometers from their workplace can no longer
reach them. At Ramallah, businesses are running on 40 percent of their
full complement of staff.

Since the establishment of Palestinian autonomy, exchanges between the West Bank and the Gaza Strip have not been encouraged. To
go through Erez, you need a specific Israeli permit. To go to the West
Bank, and therefore to cross Israeli territory, Gazans must obtain the
explicit consent of the IDF. In late 1998 the "safe passage" stipulated by
the peace agreements for linking the two Palestinian territories finally
became a reality. As its name implies, this route, open to strictly

controlled traffic, was designed more to guarantee safety to Israelis than to establish conditions under which Palestinians could come and go freely. To use the safe passage, residents of the Territories had to ask for permission from the authorities, who gave it to them on condition that they had no "security history." Departure had to be before 3 p.m., and arrival not later than 7 p.m. The coach drivers were instructed to make the journey within a given time limit, and along a set route.

In practice, the safe passage worked almost entirely in one direction. There is a regular flow of people from the Gaza Strip to the West Bank, a zone from which it is easy to enter Israel illegally and look for a job. As for West Bank inhabitants, for the most part they feel little need to enter a territory that they consider both isolated and underdeveloped.

The opening of the corridor scarcely meets the real needs of the Palestinians. There is no free access, since an authorization to travel is required as well as a modest payment. In addition to all this, the timetables and distances involved are highly restrictive: for example, to reach the departure and arrival point in Turkimiya, a village near Hebron in the West Bank, involves a lengthy detour if one is coming or going from the north. Thus there is little incentive to use the route. Furthermore, Gaza business travelers generally have a visa to go to Israel and thereafter to the West Bank. As for businesspeople from Hebron, Nablus, or Ramallah, their commercial involvement with the Gaza Strip has withered over the last few years due to the severe restrictions imposed on them. In any case, the safe passage does not apply to shifting merchandise.

To travel abroad or to emigrate, Palestinians have to do much more than obtain the requisite visa from the appropriate authorities stamped in a new passport. They have to have Israeli permission too, all exit routes being controlled by the Israeli armed services. For example, to fly abroad from Ben Gurion Airport a few miles outside Tel Aviv, one needs a visa for travel to Israel. An airport has now been built in the south of the Gaza Strip and has been in use since November 1998, but, far from offering Palestinians a means of exercising their sovereignty, it confirms their subjugation to Israel, whose armed services are in charge of security there. At the Allenby Bridge, between the West Bank and Jordan, and at Rafah, between the Gaza Strip and Egypt, Israeli forces are the ones really in charge. The Palestinian security forces who check travelers' papers are there only to save face.

THE IMPOSSIBILITY OF FREEING THE
PALESTINIAN ECONOMY

The economic agreement signed in Paris in 1995 established a kind of customs union between the Palestinian Authority and Israel: customs duties on imports were set at the same level for both, except for a range of products for which the Palestinian Authority fixes quotas according to its needs;[15] theoretically, free trade dictates commerce between the two sides. But in reality, Palestinian exports to Israel are subject to numerous restrictions. Security procedures have distorted the principles of liberalism and economic rationality, to the extent that they slow down or discourage the movement of businesspeople as well as the commercialization of their products. Moreover, the Israelis have made unilateral decisions to specify strict technical standards, and these actively prevent Palestinian products from reaching the Israeli market. Even though the rules are officially intended to protect Israeli citizens and consumers, it is evident that they also protect Israeli businesses from potential competitors.

The Palestinian economy consists of numerous small units of production. The United Nations has recorded about sixty thousand businesses in the Territories, with an average capital of twenty-five thousand dollars. Entrepreneurial activity is usually focused on the family, since the lack of a stable and defined legislative environment tends to discourage alliances that go beyond a close circle of acquaintance. In addition, banks are wary of making loans to businesspeople; the deadly uncertainty over internal and Israeli regulations, as well as over the political situation, hardly encourages investment. The political travails of the Israeli administration and the problems generated by the sealing off of the Territories further enfeeble those engaged in economic activity, who are slaves to the uncertainty of their environment.

Under these conditions, small businesses lack the means to compete with Israeli entrepreneurs who have had ample time to adapt to globalization. Palestinian businesspeople find it all but impossible to break into the Israeli market: instead, they try to maintain a strong presence in their own market, or otherwise make do with operating on a subcontract basis. Very few of them have direct dealings with foreign partners.

Most make small profits through the strong performance of Israeli commerce with the rest of the world (either by importing or exporting via Israel) and have given up the idea of developing costly and risky strategies to dominate sectors of the market. Despite free exchange agreements signed in November 1996 with the United States and in February 1997 with the European Union, the Palestinian economy is still hamstrung by its unequal relationship with Israel.

ENTREPRENEURS UNDER PRESSURE: THE EXAMPLE OF TEXTILES

The main independent production facilities for textiles and footwear in the region are in Hebron and Bethlehem on the West Bank. In Gaza, the workshops mainly do subcontracted work. Since 1994, West Bank firms have had to cut down on personnel, being unable to achieve the economies of scale necessary to increase their competitive edge and re-spond to the growing pressure to keep prices down. According to one businessman, a pair of sports shoes that he can produce for $10 can be made for $6 in China. The size of his production unit means that he must use Israeli intermediaries to buy some of his raw materials (leather, acrylic thread, polyester, and fittings), which come from Europe, Turkey, and Taiwan. A businessman from Hebron who also makes sports shoes explains: "When we want to get leather directly from abroad, we have to buy it in large quantities, an entire container-load. Now we seldom need such a large amount, so it's easier for us to buy it from Israelis who import a lot at a time."

As a general rule, Palestinian industrialists choose to import via Israel, even if the procedure is financially less viable. The length of time it takes to receive products sent from abroad and received through Israeli ports (which can take even longer at times of political tension) discour-ages Palestinian industrialists from engaging in direct commerce with their suppliers. Furthermore, if goods are held up in port due to security blocks, there are warehousing charges to be paid. So the businessman whose goods are blocked at the port or airport for security reasons is doubly penalized: he loses money because of delays to production and/or sales, and he has to pay out extra to Israeli customs.

Most locally manufactured products are sold in the West Bank. Even so, businesses do manage to send 20 to 50 percent of their goods into Israel. Commercial relations between clients in Tel Aviv are few, but usually longstanding—they go back to the early 1970s—and are based on strong links of trust. In cases where these links are broken, Palestinian businesspeople have little opportunity to forge new ones. Israel is the market in which they make the highest profit. This outlet is tending to decline under the pressure of competition from Asian counties; even Israeli textile firms are now moving their production out to Jordan or Egypt where the wages are lower. Today the textile industry, whether Israeli or Palestinian, faces a major challenge—the arrival on the market of low-price goods from China and Southeast Asia.

For representatives of these struggling businesses, is is impossible to make any inroads into the world market, especially the European one. Their place is already taken by the Israeli commercial network, which has managed to negotiate entry of their goods into European supermarket chains. Only a few Palestinians manage to export a minute proportion of their output through the intermediary of their Israeli competitors.

A new factor since the introduction of Palestinian autonomy is that for one reason or another, the Gaza Strip has become almost inaccessible. Israeli security measures have affected sales in this territory because they increase the cost of transport and pose a threat to the safe delivery of goods. The already limited financial margins possible in Gaza due to the low spending power of the population do not warrant any increased cost or effort.

In this context, measures that are officially justified by the demands of security actually reduce the capacity of Palestinian manufacturers to react fast to the needs of the market. They are weakened as a result, and this gives short-term relief to the declining Israeli sector.

PROTECTIONISM AND SECURITY

The Israeli market is theoretically accessible to Palestinian entrepreneurs, but only if they can succeed in establishing links with Israeli partners. The key factors discouraging this are the Palestinians' lack of mobility and, on both sides, suspicion. Checks made at crossing points increase delivery times and create uncertainty for the Palestinians, a particular problem for Gaza's strongly developed agricultural sector. Consignments of fruit and vegetables go bad in the heat while they are being meticulously inspected by Israeli soldiers. Then Palestinians have to deal with the problem of Israelis refusing to take checks, meaning that they must pay their suppliers in cash. And finally the Israeli Standard Institute, which is responsible for checking the conformity of all products entering Israel, makes particularly high demands on Palestinian producers in the name of quality control. A public institution, it uses technical criteria as a pretext for rejecting certain Palestinian imports, thereby unofficially protecting the Israeli producers. Palestinian food producers are also penalized when they come up against kosher requirements.

A further hindrance to trade development is the difficulty encountered by entrepreneurs in exchanges between the West Bank and the Gaza Strip. The net result is a tendency to underexploit the potential market that each could be for the other. The actual physical barriers between the two territories trouble businesspeople rather less than the constant uncertainty as to whether they will be in place on the day or not. In 1996 trade between the Gaza Strip and the West Bank was valued at no more than twelve million dollars.

The growth of trade with Egypt and Jordan remains feeble. About twenty vehicles of all types cross the frontier post at Rafah each day. In 1998, when about fourteen thousand trucks crossed between the Gaza Strip and Israel, the border crossings at Rafah were estimated at 331.[16] The total value of goods exported into Jordan was just forty million dollars, and imports did not exceed twenty-five million dollars.[17] The tariff barriers raised by neighboring Arab states[18] broadened the technical criteria imposed by the Israeli Standards Institute on any product purchased from a third country, in tandem with the security measures imposed by the Israelis,[19] have discouraged Palestinian entrepreneurs from trying to open up these markets. The fact that Palestine, Egypt, and Jordan all have similar economic profiles presents a further problem. Far from business being stimulated by the reciprocal needs of their production capabilities, they do not interact due to a protectionist attitude, which avoids the risk of competition.

Closing off the territories penalizes the Palestinians, but it also makes the autonomous zones inaccessible to Israelis. Certain Palestinians have no hesitation in taking advantage of the fears of the Israelis and their inability to come into the West Bank and Gaza Strip, by carrying on illegal commercial practices. The result is that a number of producers in Tel Aviv have complained of the sudden disappearance of Palestinian clients when payments become overdue.

A dealer in alcoholic spirits based in the suburbs of Tel Aviv accuses Palestinians of fraudulent practices: he is the sole importer of Johnnie Walker whisky, but he maintains that a Palestinian businessman has contacted his supplier to arrange a franchise. This competitor apparently intends to buy much greater quantities of the whisky than could be consumed by the inhabitants of the West Bank and the Gaza Strip. The Israeli businessman is sure that his real aim is to move the greater part of the merchandise into the Israeli state. He is convinced, what is more, that a counterfeiting business has been set up somewhere in the West Bank. In his office he has two identical bottles of whisky on show, one genuine and one an imitation.

Despite the damage done to some businesses by fraud and smuggling, the Israeli private sector remains dominant, backed by political and military decisions. If the complicity of leading economic and administrative figures can hardly be a matter of coincidence, it remains intermittent and often contradictory. Maintaining privileged access to the Palestinian consumer market is an advantage to the Israeli private sector, and the absence of any real competition from the West Bank and the Gaza Strip guarantees control of international markets. But Israeli production is mainly concentrated on high-technology products destined for the American and European markets, so that although it would be affected by the loss of the Palestinian market, the Israeli economy would not be destroyed, or even sustain lasting damage. Nor would the opening up of the Palestinian economy really endanger Israel. The Israeli economy has the dynamism and the advantages necessary to adjust rapidly to the separation of the two economies, whereas Palestinians would suffer cruelly were relations with Israel to diminish or be broken off.

FUNDING OF SECURITY BY THE ECONOMIC COMMUNITY

Despite the impression given by its numerous interventions, the state of Israel has no plan for economic domination of the Palestinian Territories. Israel's primary aim is to establish conditions that guarantee its security. In the eyes of its leaders, this aim requires the containment of the Palestinian population within their territories, to prevent acts of violence against Israeli citizens. A succession of blockades has paralyzed Palestinian economic activity, impoverished the Territories, and nurtured discontent.

Israeli experts understand that economic and social frustrations are liable to fan political violence. For this reason, they have devised security arrangements for the Territories with the aim of reconciling Israeli demands and Palestinian economic necessities. Blockades, which are criticized by the Palestinians and the international community as sporadic, abrupt, and unexpected, should be replaced by a permanent, effective, and legitimate system. The separation plan proposed by the Labor Party would set up watertight frontiers between the Territories. This plan is a response to Israel's security needs, but it is also presented as a step forward on the question of Palestinian political rights. In substance, it is saying to the Palestinians: "You wanted your own state, so now you'll have to live with closed frontiers." The decisionmakers maintain the confusion between the principle of physical separation, which corresponds to the Israeli wish to eradicate all areas of friction with the Palestinian population, that is, get rid of all links with it, and the principle of political separation that is a condition of Palestinian sovereignty. The erection of frontiers within a very limited area, where zones of sovereignty are confused, looks like a recipe for miles of extra fencing and barbed wire.

The Likud is opposed to the idea of separation for ideological reasons, because the parting of the territories will inevitably lead to the formation of a Palestinian state. However, once in power the Likud leaders did not reopen discussions on the system envisaged by the Labor Party. Fearing the impact of terrorist attacks on the electorate, the representatives of the right chose to retain the security measures.[20] So in February 2002, when the Intifada had been in existence for seventeen months,

Ariel Sharon could not keep his promise of a return to calm; his response, made in a television broadcast, was to suggest the idea of "buffer zones" along the frontiers that would "create security by means of separation and contribute to the security of all Israeli citizens."[21]

Instead of examining the causes of the violence and the future of relations with Palestine, Israel is staking all on technology. The idea is to eradicate the threat of terrorism from the Territories while avoiding penalizing Palestinian economic entrepreneurs too heavily, and to increase the security of checking procedures while making them shorter and less disagreeable. This approach aims at systematically keeping people at a distance, separated and confined—an objective hard to achieve when there is such a multiplicity of economic and commercial links across the Green Line. Complex systems will have to be introduced. The Israeli authorities, wishing to maximize efficiency in procedures and anxious to lose the stigma of an occupying power, include the Palestinian Authority in policy-making decisions. Powerless as they are to bring the discussion back to the principle of separation, the Authority's leaders negotiate its application procedures and haggle over privileges.

The logic of Israel's decision over security means that products coming from Palestinian territories must be inspected. However, the system cannot be considered coherent while the West Bank and the Gaza Strip are treated so differently. In the former, manufacturers use vehicles with Israeli license plates, whether they are making use of transport companies in East Jerusalem or whether they have set up their own transport company by using a nominee based in the Holy City. They leave trucks whose license plates betray their Palestinian origin behind in the garage, since these are not authorized to cross the Green Line; only the coveted yellow license plate avoids the risk of being checked out by the Israeli Army. In addition, the IDF is not (yet) equipped to control the entire perimeter of the West Bank. So a truck headed for Tel Aviv with a load of goods manufactured in Nablus is rarely searched. Nevertheless, checks are carried out more systematically if the goods are destined for export via Ben Gurion Airport or the port of Haifa.

Being completely enclosed, the Gaza Strip is subjected to another set of controls: virtually all traffic passes through just two border crossing points. At Erez in the north of Gaza, and at Karni in the east, the control of Palestinian exports is carried out in a different way. At Erez, Palestinian trucks loaded with merchandise are searched (the contents as well as the container). After inspection they travel in convoy to their final destination in Israel, escorted by two official vehicles carrying armed officers of an Israeli security company. The crossing point at Karni embodies the principle of separation, which has been given the status of a political solution by the Labor Party. Entirely remodeled at the end of 1999, it is the practical expression of the Israeli desire for separation and security. A high wall separates the Palestinian and Israeli territories. Openings have been made in it to allow X-ray equipment to operate. On one side Palestinians unload vehicles arriving from Gaza and place the goods on a conveyor belt. On the other side the Israelis supervise the operation, after which workers refill container trucks destined for Israel. Goods whose size makes use of the conveyor belt impossible are put into hangars, guarded only by Israelis, and undergo security checks according to procedures that are kept secret.

Trucks that travel between Gaza and Karni are licensed at Gaza. The transport of goods between the border checkpoint and their destination in Israel can be carried out in one of two ways. The first consists of using an Israeli driver and an Israeli truck. The second involves using Palestinian truckers who have been licensed by the Israeli authorities, that is, drivers who have a clean security record, and trucks that are known as "sterilized." This designation means that the truck never enters the Gaza Strip. When not in service, the truck is stationed in a parking lot, also "sterilized," on the Israeli side of the Erez crossing point.

The concept of sterilization reflects the current situation fairly accurately. On one hand, the plan is to establish separate, watertight zones, one of them considered uncontaminated and secure, the other potentially dangerous. In the light of this assumption, it becomes essential to protect the secure zone by systematically inspecting all possible points of entry from the latter. The objective is to devise and install security measures that will prove infallible. According to the Israeli officer in charge at Karni, this state of affairs has not yet been achieved, though technical refinements and increased precision should eventually allow it. On the other hand, security measures must cause minimum damage to the Palestinian economy. Instead of penalizing Palestinian truckers by banning them from making long journeys, they are hand-picked and their equipment is protected.

Ultramodern technology is expensive, and a changeover to the use of private security companies can absorb some of the cost. During weekday opening hours at Erez, a private security company is employed to inspect foreign or Palestinian vehicles leaving Gaza. At night and on the Sabbath, the IDF carries out these duties. To ensure the escort of Palestinian convoys that have crossed at Erez, the Israeli government pays nearly $500,000 each year to the security company that won the contract.

The new, up-to-date crossing point at Karni is no longer controlled by the IDF. The Israeli Airport and Port Authority (IAPA), a private company under the supervision of the Ministry of Transport, now has responsibility for the job. Although the scanners were a gift from the United States, it was this Israeli company that made the necessary investment for installing offices and constructing walls. Neither the machine maintenance costs, nor the wages of the ninety people necessary for the setup to operate efficiently, are paid by the state. Now that the company responsible for flight security at Tel Aviv Airport has taken over at Karni, the flow of goods from Gaza to Israel has become a paying proposition: a manufacturer from the Gaza Strip pays the equivalent of $76 to $115, according to the size of his vehicle, to have his merchandise inspected. Part of the cost of Israeli security is directly defrayed by Palestinian private businesses. Sixty percent of the money they hand over goes to the IAPA. The remaining 40 percent goes toward the cost of precautionary security forces on the Palestinian side of the Karni crossing point.

Today the Israeli decisionmakers have opted for the system at the Karni crossing point over the one at Erez. In the spring of 2000, the Israeli government announced that it would reserve Erez exclusively for people. All goods now have to pass through Karni. This is designed to make these new infrastructures profitable and to rationalize the principle of separation that the convoy system does not suit. Israeli logic should prevail, since the IAPA officials are planning to apply the same methods in the West Bank. All movements of human beings and goods may eventually be regulated by this system, which in the long term would lead to the sealing of the West Bank. In fact it may one day define a physical frontier to separate the two populations.

Handing over responsibility for security to the private sector shows how these inspections have become institutionalized and normalized. Measures once considered exceptional, requiring an army presence, are now carried out by a company that creates jobs, invests money in the project, and expects to make a profit. This process shows that Israeli policymakers expect a future of recurring and persistent danger, requiring fixed barriers and an adaptable business community that can respond to different needs. It also shows that the Israeli authorities mean to encourage the development of a specialized structure that will control risk in the most efficient way possible.

This system requires all the protagonists to internalize the existence of a permanent threat. The Palestinian authorities have also been involved in the development of standard inspection procedures: these have been discussed between the partners (the IAPA and Preventive Security) and sometimes renegotiated when they have proved counterproductive. The goal has been to involve the Palestinians and bring them to apply the same criteria upstream (as it were). Palestinian police officers are in daily contact with the Israelis, learning their methods and security techniques, while ordinary people involved in economic activity can forecast the time necessary for inspections into their forecasts. Security, now an integral part of the trading system, is now being financed by businesspeople who have little choice but to exchange a climate of uncertainty and slow-down for guarantees of efficiency and speed. The removal of the army makes ritual checking procedures less elaborate and significant. The aim is to make them more antiseptic. Combat gear conjures up memories of occupation, whereas civilian personnel using modern technology have a more businesslike and peaceful appearance. So the idea is also to calm the exasperated Palestinians and reduce friction between them and the Israeli authorities. Taking this logic to its conclusion, there is a plan afoot to remove the IDF presence at crossing points altogether: laser equipment capable of identifying individuals by their retina imprint would make human intervention unnecessary. This system is already in use in Southeast Asia and has great appeal for those engineering the separation.

Privatization of security makes it possible to keep an eye on potential Palestinian threats and maintain a presence at the territorial frontiers, the objective being to keep most of the population within these limits. In this way the Israeli government is moving from direct control of the Gaza Strip, which is both costly and obtrusive, to a much more sophisticated system that will be discreet, light-handed, and infallible. The Palestinian Authority has allowed the Israeli Army to shed some of its duties, in that Palestinian police have now shouldered the responsibility for repressing political groups hostile to the Israeli state. In the same way, Israel is obliging the Palestinian economic community and the international community (the Americans provide the equipment) to pay for its security.

This process of normalizing security has been altering the balance of power within Palestinian society. Incapable as they are of stopping the drive toward separation, the leaders of the autonomy are negotiating a variety of marginal concessions to protect their own short-term interests and cooperate in the management of the system being set up by the Israeli decisionmakers. This obviously confirms the authority of those in charge of security control while discriminating against the Palestinian population—whose right to free movement is unequally distributed. This new inequality is all the more marked because access to Israel is becoming the exclusive privilege of people of higher social or economic standing. Already under severe strain from its political isolation and the economic difficulties created by autonomy, Palestinian social unity is now threatened even further.

Palestinian leaders distribute VIP cards. They negotiate these with their opposite numbers in Israel, always attempting to exceed the official quota. The power to decide who benefits from VIP status allows them to control a circle of people who owe them favors or loyalty. The precious cards confer increased social status on their holders. VIPs and workers are treated very differently at the Erez crossing point; accordingly, access to Israel and the crossing procedures become directly related to an individual's socioeconomic status.

The Palestinian authorities also have a say in who receives exit permits from the West Bank or Gaza. This role as intermediary between the population of the Territories and the Israeli military naturally leads to difficulties with those who have been refused freedom of movement. The authorities can reject applications in advance either because they foresee a negative Israeli response or because they themselves do not wish to see the privilege accorded to an individual under their authority. This has two important consequences. In the West Bank it would appear that some Palestinians prefer to make their application direct to the Israeli administration, to whom they still have access, rather than to the Palestinian authorities, through which applications and permissions are usually channeled. Thus the Palestinian authorities lose the monopoly of representing those under their control. In Gaza, the situation is different: here it would appear that the Palestinian police have given up asking for exit permits. Some have even thought of exchanging their meager monthly salary for an Israeli worker's pay. In an attempt to keep them, the Palestinian authorities argue that they can't do so because they don't meet the exacting requirements of Israeli security.

INCOME GENERATED BY THE SECURITY APPARATUS

While the closure of the frontiers may have had an overall negative effect on trade, certain entrepreneurs seem to have found ways of turning the situation to advantage. Clearly the separation between Israeli and Palestinian territories is also creating new economic opportunities. The process itself involves the construction of new installations and building developments, some of which are put out to private tender. All this activity is waiting to be exploited by those who understand the requirements of security control and the way the game is played.

THE FRONTIER AS A RESOURCE

The construction of perimeter roads for the use of settlers in the West Bank was designed to put the separation between Israelis and Palestinians into practice. The work often involves commandeering plots of land from Palestinians and has invariably had the effect of reducing the size of their territory. Nevertheless, Palestinian Minister for Internal Affairs Jamil Tarifi continues to profit, directly and personally, from this state of affairs. He heads a construction company and continues to be involved in works that began under the Israeli occupation; indeed, he was the principal contractor for the IDF military bases in the West Bank. Today he is building roads that link the Jewish settlements to Israel. His business is protected by powerful circles in both Palestine and Israel.

The casino built for an Israeli clientele at Jericho in the West Bank—opposite a refugee camp—is another example of separatist policy. The construction of Oasis (as it is known) was jointly financed by Austrian capital and funds provided by members of the Authority. The staff is exclusively Palestinian, but the customers are exclusively either Israeli or foreign. Israeli citizens, forced to respect the religious requirements of their own country, flock nightly to Jericho—with or without their *kippurs*. They come by bus or drive their own automobiles, taking care to use the perimeter road reserved for them. In the parking lot, members of the Palestinian security forces speak to the visitors in Hebrew while carrying out tactful and rudimentary checking procedures. The existence of this casino gives the seal of approval to discrimination against Palestinians *by their own representatives,* by showing that there exists a class of privileged Palestinians who receive preferential treatment. Worse, it blatantly demonstrates the compartmentalization of Jews and Arabs, given that there is minimal contact between the two inside the casino. It is evident, in fact, that the former are visiting the latter simply to evade a religious taboo.

Trade between the Palestinian zones and Israel is subject to complex and bureaucratic procedures, which encourage people to bargain and make deals rather than go patiently through the system. Because these procedures interfere with the trading requirements of most businesspeople, they try all kinds of ways to get around them or turn them to their advantage. As a rule the culprits are Palestinians. Depending on what they need, they make deals with the Israeli authorities, the Palestinian authorities, and/or senior Israeli executives.

Competition is bound to impel entrepreneurs to attempt a little ad hoc rule-bending with Israeli representatives at the border posts. While the employees of the Israeli airport, the Port Authority, and the Karni crossing point look outwardly inflexible, the incorruptibility of all those involved in cross-border relations with the Palestinians cannot be guaranteed.

Palestinian businesspeople naturally do what they can to avoid the complications of Israeli bureaucracy, particularly with regard to customs. Many employ Palestinians or Arab-Israelis as intermediaries whose task is to find the best and quickest solutions to all administrative obstacles. The Palestinians are especially vulnerable to the damage that can be inflicted by a complex bureaucracy about which even the Israelis complain. Faced with a system whose logic remains a mystery to them, they must also deal with the ill will of civil servants. It follows that those Israelis or Palestinians with the necessary contacts and experience to help can sell their services. There are profits to be made.

The permits given to the Palestinians to work in Israel are bought and sold on the black market. It works in this way: taking advantage of the disarray of the unemployed and their lack of contacts for finding work at a distance, the boss of an Israeli firm, with the complicity of Palestinian acquaintances, undertakes to employ a Gaza resident. A declaration made by him to the competent authorities allows the candidate to request an exit document. As soon as he has this in hand, he can cross every morning to the other side of the Green Line to look for nondeclared jobs on his own behalf. Every month, he pays a premium to his Israeli "sponsor" as well as to the Palestinian who originally served as an intermediary.

Other illicit transactions between Israelis and Palestinians are made between individuals. The temptation for Israeli settlers to profit personally from the closure of the frontier is one example; Israeli public opinion was recently shocked by the discovery that in the spring of 2000 a young man from Gaza intent on carrying out a suicide bombing had slipped past the soldiers of the IDF in the trunk of a car belonging to a Jewish settler from the Gaza Strip.

The traffic in stolen cars also turned up some odd connivings on either side of the Green Line. Zoheir and Rami were both 21, and both were from the Balata refugee camp near Nablus. They left school at the age of 14, and for several years they specialized in stealing Israeli cars. Neither has ever held a permit to enter Israel. Yet they avoided the IDF's checkpoints and were routinely picked up by Arab Israeli confederates close to the Green Line, then taken to areas where there were not many people about. They then set about their business, breaking the headlights and sidelights of the car they wanted, so as to short-circuit its alarm. Then they broke the door lock, switched on the engine, and drove back to Nablus.

They claim to have moved two or three cars a day like that. "Down here anyone will buy a stolen car—even people working for the Authority," says Rami. The pair were never once caught or arrested by the Israeli police. Once they knocked down the owner of a car they were stealing who arrived while they were working on it and had to run. Another time, Rami spent four months in a Nablus jail for making off with a car belonging to the Palestinian envoy to the United States—an unfortunate error. Nevertheless, both young men worked at one time or another for the Authority's security services, until Rami got himself fired and Zoheir was transferred to Jericho—though he never got there because the outbreak of the al-Aqsa Intifada froze all movement between the two territories. Rami spent every penny he made; he was married with a little daughter but was content to live from day to day. Zoheir, however, invested the profits from their joint venture in a small shop in the Balata camp. As he explains: "It's quite normal for us to steal cars from the Israelis, after all the things they've done to us. We're not against peace at all—if they want to do it, we're all for it. Peace would mean we could go wherever we wanted. We could go to Amman or Tel Aviv—by car. But to go back to our grandparents' villages, well, that would be much too difficult. We'll just forget about that."

The two delinquents admire Sami, Najy, and Bassam. They made an agreement with them early on that if they came across any guns in the cars they stole, they would pass them on to the shebab. They supported what the shebab were doing to the hilt. "They're the best fighters we have. They're not like those guys who came back from Tunisia to steal the people's money. Yasser Arafat is different, of course. He's our president and we love him. When we were small, we used to cry when we saw him on TV."

The Israelis eventually cracked down on car theft. Insurance companies began insisting that people equip luxury cars with radar systems that made it possible to pinpoint them when they were stolen. Several sources claim that when one particularly valuable stolen car turned up on the West Bank, a certain former Israeli Army officer reactivated his contact with the Palestinian police chief. Together they set about recovering the vehicle for its owner, and the service thus rendered worked out cheaper than purchasing a new one. How the proceeds were divided nobody knows, but the two parties probably shared the spoils.

Another possibility shows that the roles of corrupter and corrupted can be reversed: witness the case of an Israeli firm with links to one of the Palestinian security services. Dor Energy is an Israeli company that sells gasoline; to the chagrin of its competitors, it somehow managed to pull off an exclusive contract for the export of fuel to the Palestinian Territories. This contract was signed in 1996 with one of the members of the Palestinian Authority, the deal having been assisted by a former head of Shin Beth who had gone into business on his own account. Presumably the contract carried a commission. In 1998 the scandal broke: apparently with the complicity of the Palestinian Preventive Security Force, Dor Energy had declared the sale of a quantity of gasoline in the West Bank, which it had actually disposed of in Israel. In this nefarious deal the Israeli government was swindled twice over: first when the company concealed its sales on Israeli territory, avoiding VAT, and second when the total tax on the sales declared to have taken place in the autonomous zones was refunded to the Palestinian Authority by the Israeli treasury, in compliance with the economic agreement between the two governments. Not surprisingly, legal action was brought against Dor Energy.

THE MILITARY: LEADING THE DANCE

It is no accident that the principal beneficiaries of all these business opportunities are military people. On the Israeli side, they tend to be retired generals and colonels who have set up in business. As points of contact between several spheres, they have excellent relationships in all sorts of places. Those who have served in the territories reactivate former contacts, such as Fatah activists they might have arrested earlier, but who are now part of the Palestinian power structure. These had potential as commercial partners. They might also work out an understanding with businesspeople whom they had protected during the Intifada.

The ex-officers' second advantage lies in the positions they themselves occupy within Israeli society. They have contacts not only within the political classes, but also with their still-serving military colleagues in the army and the security services. These multiple contacts give them strategic access to information. Some even have the means to impress their interests on decisionmakers, and even to lessen the various constraints to their own advantage.

Some veterans do not directly invest their energy in the Territories, preferring to sell their services as middlemen. They arrange for Israeli and Palestinian businesspeople to meet, organize the negotiations preceding contract signings, and arrange contacts with members of the Palestinian Authority. They present themselves as experts on the situation within the Territories, often because their careers have been within the civil administration that has governed the West Bank and Gaza since 1994. They also see themselves as cultural intermediaries, with the ability to decode Palestinian attitudes and declarations. They claim that the Israelis, as "Westerners," are sometimes disconcerted by the "oriental" behavior of the Palestinians. The *soi-disant* expertise of these cultural intermediaries comes from their experience, and sometimes even from their own Sephardic origins. Thus they are Arabic-speakers, either because Arabic is their mother tongue or because they have learned it to further their military careers; they know the codes of Arab courtesy, and furthermore they have a wide circle of acquaintances within the Territories. As specialists in Arab culture, they have recycled themselves as advisors.

One retired colonel who had served for thirty years in the army found an original way of coming back and using the competences he had acquired. In 2000 he set up as a tour guide for Israelis who wanted to see the Gaza Strip with their own eyes. A day trip was organized; the journey and most of the tour was made by bus, with lunch in a seaside restaurant included. The ex-officer took care, of course, to negotiate the protection of the Palestinian security services. He also had to obtain a special permission to take Israeli tourists through the Erez checkpoint, because the Israeli authorities effectively barred their citizens from entering the Gaza Strip. But the colonel, presenting himself as one who knew everything there was to be known about the region, described himself as an exceptional and impartial guide. "The problem with the Palestinian guides," he says quite seriously, "is that they hit the visitors with political propaganda." The tour of Gaza costs the handsome sum of $300 (objectivity is obviously a pearl beyond price).

On the Palestinian side, the military participants in business are all serving officers. They do not always invest directly, but they guarantee protection to certain businesspeople. Whether they are heads of security services or ordinary traders, Palestinians are greedy for contacts with the Israeli military, whose company they appreciate; they have plenty of respect for these former adversaries, whom they regard as warriors with a firm sense of honor like their own. The Palestinian military doubtless feel a certain satisfaction in their present ability to address representatives of the IDF as equals. In Gaza and the West Bank, the latter hold the keys of power and can influence decisions.

The group with the best contacts in the Israeli military and the Israeli business community consists of the chiefs of the Preventive Security Force and their allies. This police apparatus was created in the early days of Palestinian autonomy, in the spring of 1994, with the agreement of the Israeli top brass. Jibril Rajub and Mohammed Dahlan, Fatah leaders banished by the Israeli state at the outset of the Intifada, assumed the leadership of this service on the West Bank and in the Gaza Strip. Their brief was to dismantle the Islamist networks in cooperation with Israeli intelligence. The connection between the military chiefs was the last link to be broken when tension rose between the governments of the Palestinian Authority and Israel. In Gaza, Mohammed Dahlan's men occupied a strategic position. Because they were responsible for liaison with the Israeli surveillance systems at the checkpoints and in the Gaza industrial zone, they also exercised control farther up, over the Palestinian entrepreneurs, to whom they could give or withhold help. Furthermore, their presence allowed them to control the import monopolies agreed by the agents of the Palestinian Authority with Israeli firms, along the lines of the deal signed with Dor Energy. These exclusive contracts had cornered the markets in such diverse products as construction materials, certain foods, and cigarettes. The profits, estimated at between \$100 million and \$400 million,[22] have never been integrated into the budget of the Palestinian Authority. No doubt they have been used to reward the loyalty and services of people working for the government, or else to neutralize potential antagonists. And it is thought that they may have funded the Preventive Security Service, whose means have grown steadily since its foundation. The power of Dahlan and Rajub derives from the strategic alliance they have made with the economic agents of the Palestinian Authority: they guarantee the smooth functioning of their partners' affairs, and in exchange they receive a financial rake-off. Good commercial results are at the root of the security apparatus's success.[23] The cultural and diplomatic capital of all these former militants gives them additional advantages. Thanks to their forced detention in Israeli prisons prior to 1987, Rajub and Dahlan speak fluent Hebrew and are able to communicate easily with their Israeli counterparts. Their many encounters with them have created cordial and even familiar links. In this way the Palestinian military has good access to the systems of Israeli power, which they can turn to personal advantage.

The military elites on both sides of the Green Line have one major interest in common; the preservation and strengthening of their relations gives them the means to reinforce their respective positions of power. Undeniably there is a parallel between these two groups, both of which are characterized by overmighty military institutions. The proximity and density of relations between Israel and the embryonic Palestinian state encourage a process of mutual imitation and strengthening along the same lines. The central role of the respective military machines seems perfectly natural to many Palestinians, who see the Mossad or the IDF as the real power behind Israeli political decisions. This perception leads the heads of the Palestinian security services to claim major responsibilities in their country. Again, it is precisely because the Israeli military trust some of their Palestinian counterparts that the latter are able to accumulate power domestically. The strengthening of their status is one argument in favor of the idea that the generals of the Israeli Army should continue to take the lead in managing the confrontation between Israel and the Palestinians.

The Israeli state has sought to contain the Palestinians within the autonomous Territories, and to erect hermetic frontiers. Nevertheless, this project must fit in with the interconnections of the Israeli and Palestinian spaces and their economic priorities. Ironically enough, the determination of the Israeli state to engineer a divorce between Palestinians and Israelis has now become an anachronism. There will certainly be difficulties if any attempt is made to apply the Gaza separation model to the West Bank, a territory of 6,000 square kilometers with a population of 1.6 million Palestinians and 200,000 Jewish settlers located all over the zone.

The vigorous repression of the al-Aqsa Intifada has dealt a heavy blow to Palestinian sovereignty. The Israeli Army has once again invested the Territories it evacuated several years ago. While the question of political separation between the two entities is no longer at issue, the resumption of the conflict and the fears it has raised have well and truly convinced the Israeli public that living with the Palestinians is a practical impossibility. Thus the IDF has redoubled its efforts to make the movement of Palestinians into and out of Israel virtually impossible. This reinforcement of security policy has two objectives: to protect the Israeli population from acts of violence carried out by Palestinians, notably suicide bombings, and to stifle revolt within the Territories by psychologically and economically wearing down their inhabitants.

CHAPTER FIVE

Part-timers of War:
The Al-Aqsa Intifada, 2000–2002

The Israeli government claims that the outbreak of the Intifada in September 2000 was a tactic devised by Yasser Arafat to extricate himself from the political impasse he had got into by turning down the propositions of Ehud Barak at Camp David two months earlier. Ehud Barak had made unprecedented offers for the future status of Jerusalem but remained immovable on Arafat's demand that Palestinian refugees be accorded the right of return to their former homes. The Israeli prime minister was willing to concede 95 percent of the Territories occupied in 1967 and planned to group the settlements into two cohesive ensembles, which would have made inroads into the continuity of a putative Palestinian state. The Israeli political class believes today that the head of the PLO was unable to decide on a negotiated solution and so preferred to gamble on a military-type victory so as to strengthen his own legitimacy and charisma in the eyes of his own side. While it is true that Arafat can occasionally win dividends from popular revolt, this analysis denies the national aspirations of Palestinian society. The explosion of violence in September 2000 showed the bankruptcy of the system of territorial and political control that Israel had tried to impose on the Palestinians, as well as the refusal of the Palestinians to bow to it. Moreover, the al-Aqsa Intifada heralded the return of the shebab, along with their determination to occupy the forefront of the scene. Frustrated in their aspirations of progress within society and tired of a system of power and redistribution that offered them nothing but crumbs, the militants called the foundations of the social and political order back into question. While the shebab tended to escape the control of the Palestinian Authority, they still had none of the advantages they needed to be successful in their undertaking.

The return to violence did not necessarily translate into total intransigence vis-à-vis Israel; in some ways, the Fatah militants were pragmatic, which was certainly not the case with the generation of "little brothers." All this illustrated the growing disarray and radicalization of a people frustrated in the acquisition of their sovereignty.

THE FIGHTER AND THE ARTIST

"Of course I'll accept a Palestinian state that includes the West Bank, Gaza, and Jerusalem. You could hardly dream of more. If they'll respect us, we'll respect them. If they want peace, if they give us peace, we'll give them peace back. I agree with Gaddhafi: if Israel gives the Palestinians their rights, the Arab world will no longer view Israel as its enemy. If the Israelis accept us, I'll be very happy to place them at the head of the Arab League."

Muffled up in his bomber jacket, with his pistol and his cell phone stuck in his belt, Sami grinned as he threw out this daring proposal to welcome Israel into the Arab world. As a Fatah militant, imprisoned and banished by the Israeli authorities before returning in the slipstream of the Palestinian Authority, Sami took up arms against the IDF once again in October 2000. There was no hatred in his ideas, more a conviction that he had been comprehensively duped. Since 1993, the Jewish settlement perched on the hills around Nablus had been steadily spreading; all movement within the West Bank, like travel abroad, had remained firmly under Israeli control. The occupation had not ceased; on the contrary, it was continuing to affect the daily lives of Palestinians as well as their minds. Sami added: "I'd like to see a country where every child has rights. I'd like to be able to go wherever I like, like anybody else in the world. I want a country without war and without weapons—like Switzerland. Of course that won't happen in my lifetime, but maybe my children will see it."

Najy's position wasn't much different. He had no problem with Israel's existence, even though he had been quite prepared to kill Israeli Army troops ever since the start of the al-Aqsa Intifada. He had met a few Israelis. Apart from the members of the prison administration he had to deal with between 1985 and 1990, he took part in a number of encounters organized with Israeli Labor Party members, and he got on with them quite well. Like Sami, Najy was barred from leaving the West Bank; he could not go to Gaza or Israel or anywhere else in the world. The Israeli security forces took the view that the two men's activist past was just too heavy. And yet the shebab weren't ready to throw in the towel yet. Najy claimed that he could go to Tel Aviv whenever he liked. "I've got no permit, but I can do without, I don't care. I go across in the night. Tel Aviv is beautiful."

Najy and Sami made enough money to go to Israel with friends once in a while and have a good time. Najy claimed they could spend several thousand shekels in an evening if they chose, just for the fun of roaming around a town they weren't allowed to enter. Crossing the Green Line unscathed was an experience that took them back to the fear and the thrill of their former clandestine activities. The lure was one of pure pleasure, of escaping the prison of Nablus for a while, of having fun and spending money like the Israelis, because pleasure wasn't reserved for Israelis alone. Sami told how on one occasion they went to a rather special club. The entrance fee was exorbitant, but it covered everything—dinner, drinks, and women, as many as you liked. Najy liked to get drunk from time to time, but he wouldn't go with the girls. "Personally," he said, "if it's just to go in and out, no thanks. I can't imagine making love to a woman if I haven't kissed every inch of her from top to toe."

Aziz has known Najy, Sami, and Bassam since he was a small boy. Today he doesn't know how to handle guns; instead he spends his time falling in and out of love and testing out his artistic talents. Aziz is also a child of the Balata camp. When Aziz was eight, his father fell ill and had to give up earning a living in Israel. His mother took over and worked as a cleaner for a Nablus family. His elder sister looked after Aziz and his younger siblings. All the children went out to work when they weren't at school; they scavenged around the workshops for aluminum and sold it to sheet metal workers. Aziz was a quiet child who never got into fights, even when the others aggressed him. He remembers how his mother took him with her when she went begging. With his hand clasped in hers, he followed her from door to door around the middle-class districts of Nablus. "For me, the whole world boiled down to Balata. Nablus, only five minutes away, was another planet and it scared me. One day, we went to the house of a man who gave me sweets. He tried to take advantage of my mother, but we got out of there and I left the sweets behind. I knew what we were doing was wrong, but I had to tag along. When I was small, I prayed and wondered why our lives had to be that way. When I asked my mother, she just said shut up. Once she asked me to go and buy a dish of *foul* (cooked broad beans) for break-fast. I went to the shopkeeper, a fat guy who spluttered when he spoke. I told him my dad would pay that evening. The man just said, no money, no *foul*. When I got home my mother cried."

Aziz has no idea if the *foul* seller was a hard-hearted man, or whether he meant to teach him a lesson. In any case, he drew the conclusion that there was no sense in living off other people. Today, when he sees a poor child, he doesn't dispense money—or pity, either. As a child, he loathed the compassion of adults. "They say the poverty here is a consequence of the occupation, but it's not true," he says. Aziz has stopped going to the mosque and has abandoned the Muslim faith.

When Israel invaded Lebanon in 1982, Aziz began working in the Shabiba. He founded a group in the camp, along with Bassam. In 1986, at sixteen, he went to prison for two years. Under the tutelage of Fatah, he studied and took part in political discussions and sports. Whenever he had any free time, he read poetry or history. He also wept. He got out of prison just as the Intifada was getting under way, but he was careful this time—he didn't want to go back to jail. When a special unit came in to crush the political and military activities of Bassam's group (see chapter 1) and shot Khaled right in the middle of the Balata refugee camp, Aziz saw the whole thing. "I was leaning against a wall talking to someone and I saw the special forces come in. One of them shot Khaled in the leg. I saw the bullet go through his pants. I wanted to go in there, into the wound to feel what it was like. Then they fired at him again and I wondered how the soul leaves the body. I just watched and said noth-ing: the gunshots, the people yelling. They killed him in cold blood, just

like that, like they were squashing an insect. At that moment I under-
stood that in just the same way we Palestinians were convinced that
Palestine belonged to us, the Israelis were quite certain it was theirs."
Aziz went home and wrote a poem.

Later, he was teaching the *dabka* to a group of girls. In the middle
of a lesson, the Israeli Army tossed a tear gas grenade into the room
where they were practicing. Two of the girls passed out. "This was my
first real experience as an artist, and the occupiers were trying to stop
me making a success of it. Then I realized I could fight them with art."
After failing to win a study grant abroad, he signed up at the Fine Arts
School of Nablus University in 1993. He worked and studied in tandem
for seven years.

Aziz eventually obtained a permit to work in Israel, where he found
a job in a clothes factory. He got on well with his Israeli fellow workers,
since nobody bothered to talk politics. Nevertheless, he sometimes de-
tected the latent hatred between Jews and Arabs. A Moroccan Jewish
woman took a liking to him because he reminded him of her son, who
had stayed behind in Morocco. She cooked for him and gave him small
presents. "It was nothing political. It was just human, natural sympathy
between us. If she'd had some kind of political agenda, or if she'd meant
to give some kind of good impression of the Israelis to the Palestinians,
I could never have accepted the relationship," says the artist from
Balata. At the factory, he fell in love with a young Israeli girl, Sophia,
who was already involved with another colleague. Aziz nursed his pla-
tonic passion and showed his love as best he could. But the day he had
to say goodbye to her he wept bitterly (though not in her presence).

Ever since the formation of the Palestinian Authority, Aziz has
done his best to make a living from his gifts as an artist. He has formed
theater groups, written plays, taught theater and the *dabka* to Balata
children. He refuses to subscribe to exchanges with the Israelis. He had
an offer to direct a play about friendship between Israelis and Palestinians but felt that it was a play by the Israelis to serve their own political
ends. "If they really want to acknowledge our rights, they should get out
of our country! They should go back to where they came from."

Aziz would like to return to his grandfather's village near Jaffa. The
house is still there, with its apple trees. "When I go back to the Palestine
of 1948, my heart beats more strongly—the air has a special quality up

there," he remembers. At one point he even considered marrying an Is-raeli Palestinian girl so he could go there to live, adopt Israeli national-ity, and buy back his family home or at least find somewhere to live in the village. But in the end he abandoned the notion as being too indi-vidualistic. He still plans to marry one day, though not with the woman he loves, who is already the mother of another man's family. He'd like an educated wife who could teach their children—two or three at most. Aziz would prefer daughters "because they need their father more, they're much more attached to the family." And also because he's in mortal dread of a son of his getting killed.

"In some ways I like the occupation, because it has made us learn the value of our country, which has led us to love our own people. Bassam, Sami, and Najy chose to take up arms. I chose a different road," he declares. When, in 2001, his friends fired on the IDF, he felt that it was a useless gesture. As far as he can see, the only effective tactic today is the suicide bombing.

LOVE AND POLITICS

Sami lives in a ground floor bedroom of his family's house. The former camp hovel has been transformed. Almost every year, a new floor gets built to lodge yet another married brother. Sami himself would like to buy a house somewhere outside the camp, outside the town, on a hill maybe, way out in the country. He'd live there with Iman, whom he has always loved. Several times she almost slipped out of his grasp, and Oc-tober 2000 would certainly have been the moment to ask her to be his wife, if he hadn't had to put his personal sentiments aside yet again to join the Intifada. It was as if the struggle against the Israelis was fated to destroy his entire life.

Iman is the youngest in a stalwart Fatah family. Her education was a liberal one for a camp girl. Because she had health problems, her father was inclined to pamper and spoil her, and he encouraged her to take no notice of what people thought of her. He bought her a bike, something usually reserved for boys.[1] He also encouraged her to study, to think rationally, and to ignore superstitious beliefs. During the In-tifada, he showed her that personal education was the most important advantage in dealing with the enemy. Her militancy would be all the more effective if she could be a successful student. And so it proved: Iman was a good student and was elected to the Shabiba in her school. She took part in demonstrations and on one occasion was hit in the legs by rubber bullets, which made walking impossible for several days. She took her exams when the Intifada ended. During one of them, masked shebab burst into the room and scrawled the answers on the blackboard, the idea being to deliver the examinees from a test that had been unjustly imposed on them at a troubled time of occupation and revolution. The test was annulled and Iman did not receive her diploma. The following year she decided to take it all over again as a free candidate, but this plan was abandoned for good after a visit to her brother abroad. She now works as a secretary in a government office.

At twenty-seven, Iman is still single and wonders if that's the way she'll stay. She has received many offers of marriage. Rami, her first suitor, was a neighbor a few years older than she. Iman, a pretty, diminutive creature, was afraid of him—later, she said she never really fancied him. Rami came by regularly with his mother to press his suit, but every time Iman turned him down. She was friends with his sisters, however, and once, when she had stayed late at their house, she saw Rami surreptitiously picking some of her hair off a cushion on which she had rested her head. She took the gesture as a sign of absurd devotion, but it turned out to be just the opposite—another side of Rami, the patient if fetishistic lover, was revealed when she found out he had used the hairs to put a hex on her. He mixed the hairs with dirty liquid, placed them in a jar with a short page of writing condemning Iman to a life of celibacy, and slipped the whole mess into a wall-cranny in her house. The first effects of this surfaced when Iman, in a moment of complete abstraction, suddenly accepted the proposal of her indefatigable neighbor. She quickly thought better of it, but her family was at a loss to explain the sudden change of heart. Her elder sister advised her to consult a Samaritan.[2] But Iman, faithful to her dead father's teaching, refused to give in to superstition. As far as she was concerned, her uncertain future and her anxieties were plain bad luck.

When Sami was in Jordan, his brother came to ask Iman to marry him. So did plenty of other shebab from the Balata camp and elsewhere. Iman finally settled on a young man she didn't know, the brother of her best friend who had gone to live in the United States. The two signed a marriage contract in front of the *imam* and brought their families together for a small party, knowing quite well that the union would not be consummated until the marriage ceremony. The groom left for the United States, while Iman stayed behind, vainly trying to obtain a visa. The future husband suggested they circumvent the legal procedure and attempt another route. Iman didn't like this idea; if she went to the United States as an illegal alien, she would never get back to see her family until her situation was put to rights. Moreover, this huge, distant country was far from attractive to her. She would rather go on living in the Balata camp. Despite her family's opposition, Iman decided to break off the marriage. It was effectively a divorce, since a marriage contract had been signed. Her elder brother, her legal guardian, went with her before the judge.

Iman was in love with Sami, but she was afraid her family would stop her marrying him. Sami was out of work; on the face of it, his life was unstable. He risked losing his life. He knew he should organize his future, but the new Intifada had caught up with him, distancing him even further from his personal project of settling down.

Why was he risking his life again? Perhaps on account of a habit that neither he nor Najy nor Bassam had ever managed to shake off. Having been exposed to harsh repression, having been participants in a clandestine struggle, their natures had been molded by violence. Their early experience of it made them unsuitable for other roles. Sami, for example, had no professional activity and his love life was uncertain, to say the least. As he said himself, "At thirty years of age, what with the Israeli occupation, I have no house of my own and I can't get married." And yet Sami wasn't short of money. Perhaps his inability to steady himself was linked to certain psychological barriers. The way he expressed it, he couldn't imagine devoting himself to his own personal life until the Palestinian Territories had freed themselves from Israeli domination. But even though the Israeli state's occupation affected Palestinian daily life in scores of ways, it did not stop people getting married—at least those people who didn't need to cross a frontier to do so. If Sami didn't manage to carry through his project of marrying Iman, it was either because he felt he couldn't both fight the enemy and found a family, or else because he thought it indecent to enjoy life as long as the Israeli occupation continued. He had real difficulty in individualizing his own destiny, in disconnecting it from the fate of his country and the cause he was defending.

For many young people, the collective political failure is the mirror of their own shipwreck. By adopting this posture, they can decline all responsibility for their own lack of success and blame the occupying power for their personal misfortunes. The way they see it, the Israeli military domination that proscribes Palestinian sovereignty invades every aspect of their lives, right down to the most intimate detail. This perception leads some young Palestinians to adopt an attitude of resignation, as if they were declining to be the prime movers in their own existence.

To escape this fate, one of the more attractive options is to leave, to go abroad. In this sense, happiness and the projection of oneself into the future are only to be contemplated if one is prepared for a clean break with one's social and national milieu. Fuad, a friend of the group, put it succinctly: "All I know how to do is start fights and shoot people. I don't know how to do anything else. I want to go to the USA and never set foot in this place again. When I get there I'll settle down and work like everyone else." Fuad was clear-eyed about his total inability to achieve anything for himself as long as he stayed in Nablus—except oscillate between the roles of freedom fighter and street thug. On the other hand, once he got somewhere else, away from the old environment, he believed he would be able to assume a "normal" life, to buckle down to the constraints of hard work and hard effort. That was how he measured his destiny: either he managed to get out, or else he died in the current Intifada. He had amassed enough money to organize his departure and invest in something once he reached his final destination. Also he had friends in the United States who could help him. All this seemed plain enough, even though he didn't speak a word of English and believed himself incapable of doing anything but "shoot guns and cause trouble." Yet in America, "everything would be so completely different." The obstacle, and it was a huge one, was getting a permit to leave the West Bank, which the Israelis would never give him on account of his militant history. And as long as they were stuck where they were, neither

Fuad nor Sami nor Najy would feel that they were truly alive unless they were using their weapons. The insuperable difficulty for them was to find another means of affirming themselves.

As for Najy, he decided several years ago not to seize an opportunity for emigration that presented itself. At that time he met a Canadian girl, and although his English was almost nonexistent and her Arabic not much better, they set up house together. After a few months, she suggested that they return to Canada together. She had a place for them to live, and she could take care of him. Najy hesitated; he knew quite well that this would change his life completely. He bought a plane ticket, then went back on his decision. Somehow he had an intuition that he was incapable of achieving anything in this distant land. "I've never worked in my life," he said. "There's nothing I can do." His frank fear of the unknown shows that, despite the strength of his longing to leave, the dread of losing his bearings was even stronger. For some young people the dilemma is quite simply insoluble: it's impossible to live here, while to try and live anywhere else—even if you do manage to surmount all the obstacles to getting there—is like tearing out your soul. So Najy decided to stay behind and start a family in the Territories.

When the new Intifada broke out in the fall of 2000, Najy stopped spending his nights with his wife. His renewed clandestine existence took him even farther away from home. On several occasions Leila threatened to leave him and go back to her family, but she never has. Najy loved his wife and daughters; he provided for them, and yet sometimes he hit the nail on the head when he considered his inability to fully assume the role of father and husband. "It would be better," he said, "if I just left them a pile of money and died." Death is one of the few possible ways out, the eventual price of combat, the escape hatch from pain and disappointment.

Bassam seemed to find it easier to build a life of his own, to plan a future that firmly removed him from the war zone. By studying sociology with the aim of finding work in the social development sector, he provided himself with the wherewithal to effect a genuine change in his life. He was a little older than the others, and he was not quite as young as they were when he was first exposed to the harshness of Israeli repression. As a practicing Muslim, his strictly personal religious faith gave him more ways of structuring his life. In any event, out of solidarity with the others and out of personal conviction, he rejoined the struggle shoulder to shoulder with them.

The role of fighter, which has stayed with every member of the group so tenaciously, was also imposed from the outside—in particular by the Israeli Army, which singled them out early on as dangerous activists. Knowing, or sensing, that they were liable to be arrested or even eliminated, they felt that if they had to risk their lives they would rather do it on the battlefield. The IDF, conducting its repression-by-anticipation, created the circumstances for the remobilization of the shebab. From this standpoint a phenomenon reemerged that was already a powerful factor at the time of the first Intifada, namely, a shift to clandestinity leading directly to taking up arms. In the late 1980s, when the militants found out that they were about to be arrested they instantly separated into armed groups and went into hiding.

Ali is a friend of Najy's, whom he got to know in prison during the early 1990s. He lives in a refugee camp close to Ramallah. During the first Intifada, his brother was cut down by a hail of bullets, his family's house was destroyed by the IDF while he was on the run, and he was wounded on three occasions. As the head of an armed group formed in 1988, he was caught and sentenced to life imprisonment two years later. Freed in 1999, he found a job in the Ministry for Prisoners. A loyal Fatah militant, Ali supported the Oslo accords in the belief that they would lead to the establishment of a Palestinian state and the end of the conflict with Israel. Today, he acknowledges that the strategy has failed and reproaches the Palestinian leaders for bad management and corruption. He feels that the shebab of the 1987 uprising have been cheated, insofar as they obtained no political satisfaction and won no personal recognition. "Look at me," he says. "I spent fifteen years of my life behind bars, and here I am now in a microscopic office with three other guys. I earn 1,500 shekels a month [about $450 dollars]."

Why should he go back to the fight at this stage? There is nothing in Ali's attitude of vengefulness against the system that has wronged him, nor any personal strategy aimed at raising his status because he took part in the struggle. He explains: "It's true enough that people sacrifice themselves and exhaust themselves. And I don't expect to be made a minister tomorrow. I know I'll go on being cornered like a rat in

Ramallah, and that they [the people in the Palestinian Authority] will go on traveling wherever they like. What's really important to me is victory over the Israelis. Fighters sacrifice themselves and risk their lives. But whether or not we take part in the actual fighting, our lives are always on the line. Last week, a woman going home with her children was hit by a bullet. I could be hit by a bullet, too, or happen to be somewhere when a bomb goes off. In the circumstances we may as well fight. In any case, the Israelis have been after me ever since this Intifada began."

Even though Ali is convinced that the Intifada is justified, he shows that his own career and the person he has become propel him inexorably toward armed struggle. The role of resistance fighter prepared to put his body on the line for the fatherland is the only one he really knows. The pressure of the Israeli Army is also a trigger factor. Because he senses the precariousness of his existence, he is ready to run extra risks.

For a certain number of young people, the opportunity of a fresh uprising against Israel has allowed them to return to an earlier status and savoir-faire within society. Even when they are part of the Palestinian administration, they can still feel marginalized. Some, like Najy and Sami, have had trouble finding their bearings within the context of civil peace. But the imperfect social integration of these young people is far from the only reason for their dissatisfaction and sense of being out of step. The way the Palestinian government has operated since the formation of the Authority has provoked a feeling of injustice among some of the shebab of the Intifada. Most of them have lowly jobs in the hierarchy and have scarcely had a taste of the material advantages that come with power. Their personal position in relation to the new political order encourages them to risk change. They also think that the peace process into which their leaders have drawn them has not fulfilled its earlier promise, and that their negotiators caved in to unacceptable Israeli demands. In this context, the uprising is viewed as a necessity, for breaking with a policy of submission and compromise. The Palestinian Authority is on the wrong track and lacks the tools it needs to stand up to the Israeli state. Popular mobilization must compensate for these perceived weaknesses. Najy was all for the agreement. "I thought it would turn us into a state, but it turned out like Antoine Lahad.[3] Anyone who takes a shot at the Israelis gets arrested. I'm against that, and that's why I resigned from the Preventive Security Force. Abu Ammar is surrounded by people who put pressure on him."

The regime's discredit has generally spared Yasser Arafat. The Fatah shebab are still loyal to their chief, and very few of them are ready to call his leadership in question. To explain his errors, they point to his entourage or to the pressures exerted on him by foreign powers. This attachment to Arafat's person, this determination not to blame him, probably derives from a wish to preserve some kind of certainty about things. People's disappointment with the failure of the Palestinian national project and with the political classes already runs very deep. Likewise there has been disenchantment with the heads of the PLO as representatives of the Palestinian people; those men, condemned to exile for decades past, are perceived today more as profiteers than patriots. The hostility of many shebab toward the Palestinians from abroad, the members of the Authority, illustrates the deepening rifts within Palestinian society. Sami's reaction shows that in his eyes the PLO apparatchiks belong to a category that is no longer worthy of the nation. "When they were abroad, we thought they were good people. In fact when they came back, they did it to do business and make money. They're not like us at all, they're out for themselves. They know all this can't last so they're doing deals and investing in foreign countries because they're planning to get out of here."

DISSENSIONS AND THE INTIFADA

People who are nostalgic about the first Intifada are banking on another full-fledged uprising to reunite Palestinian society around its national objectives. In reality, the confrontations that have been gathering since September 2000 do not look anything like the mass civil disobedience that shook the Territories in the late 1980s. Very rapidly, divergences of opinion and interests reappeared among the population. As in December 1987, the al-Aqsa Intifada began with a popular explosion in reaction against an Israeli act that was seen as deliberately provocative. Young people assaulted the Israeli military camps, pelting them with stones, and the battles quickly spread throughout the Territories. During the first

Intifada, political formations seized on the people's spontaneous fury and structured it into a movement of struggle. The definition of a political line, along with clear goals and modes of action, kept the movement going and allowed it to include entire sections of the population. In 2000 the rage and despair of adolescents who were ready to meet bullets with stones yielded to groups of militants who were armed but ill-coordinated and not very effective. The battle essentially consisted of confrontations between professional soldiers armed with ultrasophisticated weapons, and shebab with M16 rifles and grenades. While the fighters now had light weapons, they had very little room for maneuver. To begin with, the geographic imprisonment of the Palestinians whose towns and villages were besieged by the IDF restricted their capacity to use guerrilla warfare. Again, the existence of a national authority has deprived them of any autonomy in making decisions, to such a point that no simple political structure has been able to take effective command of the Intifada. The political heads of the movement are still bound by the decisions and orders of Yasser Arafat. Finally, the Israeli repression has gradually exhausted Palestinian society's capacity to endure.

In the first weeks of the Intifada in 2000, Najy and Sami decided that it was time to give up distractions and frivolities. They went to town and set fire to the two alcohol outlets in Nablus, taking the pledge to renounce drink themselves. The entire population, according to them, should be behind them in this initiative. With martyrs dying for the cause, national cohesion required that there should be no hint of festivity. The restaurants of Nablus lost their clientele practically overnight; the tables weren't empty because there was no money, but because the richer families understood that it would be wiser to stay home.

In certain quarters, it was no longer safe even to do that, for a whole section of the population now found itself caught between the guns of the shebab and those of the Israeli Army. People were not slow to manifest their dissatisfaction with this state of affairs. In April 2001 a petition was sent to the governor of the Nablus region. The signatories demanded that the armed militants cease forthwith to organize their operations from within the town. The position of these families was comforted by the Palestinian Authority's decision to forbid all shooting in the zones designated A, over which it exercised civil and military control.

From the tactical standpoint, shooting at Israeli outposts was ineffective, and throughout the first year of the Intifada the shebab were unable to touch the soldiers, who wore bulletproof vests and helmets and stayed behind highly effective protective systems. The harassment technique yielded very few results; indeed, it allowed the Israeli Army to justify its presence and the repression it was carrying out. Nor did the Israeli troops hesitate to fire back on civilian targets.

Even in the entourage of the Balata shebab, a certain number of veterans of the first Intifada were critical of what was going on. Anwar, who had belonged to Fatah since the 1980s, was expelled from the Territories in 1990 and took advantage of his exile to carry out sociological and demographic studies. He had been born at the refugee camp and now worked in Ramallah, where he ran a youth center. Although he was still friends with the fighters, his analysis favored a different approach to theirs. "As far as I'm concerned, what's happening today is not an Intifada at all. If the Israelis raise the siege, there'll be no more Intifada. There's no unified command, no program, and no real coordination between the different political forces. Unity only exists in the eyes of the media, and in the figure of Marwan Barghuti. But he's not the one who is organizing and directing the uprising. The 1987 Intifada was a complete system, which ruled our lives. And the objective of the movement was clear. Today nobody knows what we want. I'm not really in favor of military combat. The Israelis want this kind of confrontation, but we shouldn't: we don't have the means. The best way is to work on ourselves, get rid of corruption, build our institutions. If we had a parliament that really worked, and a strong democracy, now *then* we'd be in a position to take on the Israelis."

In Najy's view, what was hampering the Intifada was the attitude of the leading families. According to him, the notables were falling away because it was in their interest to maintain a climate of peace so as to keep their business affairs going. They had nothing to gain from a resumption of hostilities, or from the return of the shebab to the forefront of the scene. "They're against the Intifada because in any case they have money and they can go to Tel Aviv. Not one of their sons is taking part in the Intifada. We never saw any of them in jail. Ghassan Shaka's son has been in the U.S. ever since it started."

Najy was wrong on at least one count: in early 2001 the son of General Mahmud al-Allul, a member of a prominent Nablus family and the governor of the township, was seriously injured by Israeli Army bullets in the course of a demonstration. The involvement of the governor led to unaccustomed solicitude on the part of the Israelis, who sent in an IDF helicopter to evacuate the child to an Israeli hospital. To no avail: the boy died of his injuries.

Even when the fighting was at its fiercest, contacts were maintained between the Palestinian leaders and their Israeli counterparts. At the local level, exchanges took place among the governor, the mayor, and the Israeli commander of the northern region of the West Bank. These contacts might eventually have been used for more personal business, but it seems that for the moment their objective was to defuse tensions on the ground. In effect, the representatives of the Authority—all notables of the town—also had the option of liaising with the shebab. Thus Ghassan Shaka and Mahmud al-Alul called in Najy, Sami, and Bassam at the outset of the new Intifada and negotiated to stop them attacking the IDF from within Nablus. Najy described the interview: "They asked us to come. Ghassan Shaka said to me: 'You know, you worry me because you shoot first and ask questions after.' I told him I'd be glad to wait for him to give the order to shoot, if I thought he ever would."

In any case, Bassam, Sami, and Najy suspended attacks on the IDF, but the agreement was tenuous. According to their evaluation of the situation on the ground and the state of their relationship with the town's notables, the shebab might go back on the offensive at any time against the Israeli Army.

In December 2000 the police in Nablus decided to confiscate and burn all cars known to have been stolen in Israel. The official reason for this was that the young thieves who were profiting from the traffic and driving stolen vehicles around were behaving in an unruly, irresponsible way on the roads. The real goal, of course, was to reduce the shebab's room for maneuver by physically immobilizing them. Najy's car went up in smoke; Sami, by the skin of his teeth, managed to sell his just before it was impounded. Najy immediately resigned from the police force, then rejoined a few months later: after this he was allowed to keep a small car (also stolen in Israel), provided it was painted with police markings. Meanwhile a warrant was issued for his arrest, but no arm of the military was particularly eager to execute the order. "Let them try!" crowed the hero of al-Najah University. "They'll never get into Balata!" And it was true: any intrusion of the sort would provoke the rage of ordinary people and mobilize the entire population of the camp. So Najy went to work as usual, marched into the police chief's office, and brazenly settled into his chair.

In some ways, the balance of power and authority had been turned upside down. The police boss implicitly acknowledged that relations with the shebab oscillated between fear and control. His way of dealing with the shebab was to use the technique of carrot and stick. While he was ready to intervene and deprive them of the stolen cars in their possession, their traffic in guns (also mostly stolen in Israel) went unpunished. And Najy and Sami made a significant part of their living from dealing in arms. In this way they made sure they themselves had more than enough weaponry, while keeping other groups supplied as well.

Although the Intifada was an opportunity for the shebab to recover the power and status they had lost in recent years, it was far from certain that they would prevail in any trial of strength within their own society. They were being inexorably squeezed.

Yasser Arafat, having chosen the path of political negotiation, was exposed to Israeli demands and under pressure from the international community. He had no way of taking the initiative in the struggle—indeed, it was his presence more than anything else that prevented the formation of a unified command along the lines of the first Intifada. Under the circumstances, the Palestinian Authority was tempted to stake all on the preservation of its international credit, at the expense of the support of the shebab. The Authority was exposed to political and military pressure from the Israelis and the Americans that placed it in a false position vis-à-vis its own people. The national Palestinian struggle had had much greater latitude when the PLO was based abroad.

As for the IDF, it plodded on with its policy of systematically eliminating Palestinian activists. The methods varied. In June, Fuad was picking up some guns he'd bought at the northern end of the West Bank when his car blew up. The driver was killed instantly and Fuad was injured. A few weeks later, Najy narrowly escaped a similar attack when he surprised some men placing a bomb under his own car. That fall a booby trap exploded in the office of Jamal Mansur, the Islamist leader in Nablus. It killed six people—four Hamas members and two Palestinian journalists who happened to be in the room. The IDF regularly bombed the premises of the various security services in reprisal for Palestinian forays.

Despite the atmosphere of high tension, Najy advised his friend Sami to get his love life settled once and for all by formally asking Iman to be his wife. Sami agreed to do so, and in company with the trusty Bassam and Najy he paid a visit to Iman's brothers. They had no objection to the match. It was agreed that if the military situation allowed, the wedding would be celebrated sometime during the summer. But in August 2001, when Sami, Najy, and a few other shebab were strolling down a narrow street in old Nablus, their group was struck by a missile. Some children nearby were slightly hurt. Iman seems to have been right when she called herself ill-starred: Najy was hit in the leg, Sami in the head. A doctor was rushed out from Jerusalem, but nothing could be done to save Sami, who died soon after.

Now the situation of the shebab grew more and more precarious with each passing day. Differences between the Palestinian Authority and the Intifada militants had become acute. In December 2001 Yasser Arafat's speech at Aid, the feast marking the end of Ramadan, raised the hackles of Najy and Bassam. The PLO leader seemed to be caving in to Israeli and American demands by calling for an end to the violence. Once again the Balata shebab found themselves at loggerheads with the Palestinian security services, which were intent on putting them behind bars. Nevertheless, a compromise was worked out. Bassam was placed under house arrest, while Najy contrived to live on in hiding, in terror of the IDF on the one hand and of the Palestinian intelligence services on the other. He became a practicing Muslim, praying fervently five times a day.

THE YOUNGER BROTHERS

Haloed with the aura of their generation, the shebab of the first Intifada believe today that the post-2000 class of young men are woefully short on political awareness, with a tendency to duck the battle against Israel. They explain their juniors' lack of fight by their absence of political or educational training. Sami used to say of the younger brothers "they don't know much about Palestine and the nation. They hardly even did primary school because the curfews during the Intifada kept them at home." Nevertheless, the feeling is that today's twenty-year-olds are lucky to have been in their teens during the first flush of Palestinian autonomy, what with the traffic in stolen cars, the drugs, the lure of restaurants and discothèques, the forays into Israel and its forbidden pleasures.

This view of the younger generation implies not only a comparison with the senior shebab's experience, but also a way of giving extra weight to their own political engagement. The older ones set great store by the respect they had won in the battle against Israel, and in the preservation of the group to which they belonged. Today the shebab of the first Intifada are disinclined to pass on their battle know-how to their juniors, whom they consign to less important activities. Sami always felt they shouldn't take part in military operations. "They're just too young. They do street demonstrations instead."

Still, plenty of adolescents dream of distinguishing themselves in the heat of battle. Mansur comes from the Balata camp; he knows Najy and Bassam and admires them, just as he admired Sami before he was killed. At eighteen, he has already been working for seven years full time to feed his seven brothers and sisters, filling the role of his father, who had to give up a laborer's job in Israel because of ill health. He has had some experience in handling weapons, having worked for a few months with the Preventive Security Force. "I tried to join the shebab who were taking pot-shots at the Israelis," he says. "But they didn't want me. I don't know why—I can handle a gun. Maybe they're just scared of newcomers because of the risk they might get penetrated by a collaborator. It's a mystery to me. In any case, I can't assemble a group of my own, single-handed."

Although today's younger Palestinians are good at knocking off cars and finding their way to sources of forbidden pleasure, delinquency is certainly not the rule among them, as is commonly thought. The spread of delinquency in the Territories in the 1990s was more a reflection of the way society in general was moving, for the end of the Intifada and the setting up of some form of national sovereignty were followed by a real relaxation of moral strictures in the Territories. The end of the absolute requirement for combat authorized a greater measure of access to amusements and pleasure, which the population had hitherto sternly renounced for the duration of the first Intifada. As for the traffic in stolen Israeli vehicles, this was steeply on the increase because the now-autonomous Territories had become far less accessible to the Israeli population and the Israeli Army. In this illicit trade, young people of about twenty tended to be the stooges of far older ringleaders.

The charge of laxity and indifference made against the younger generation hardly chimes with its puritanical bent, so encouraged by the rigorous moral atmosphere of the Intifada. After all, in 1994, twelve-year-old children were the ones pelting unveiled women with stones in the working-class areas of Gaza.

In Balata, the reactions of Yussef are less violent, though perhaps more revealing. Yussef is a shy youth of eighteen who refuses to shake the hands of women and dares not look them frankly in the eye. He's a devout Muslim and an obedient son who respects the precepts of his mother. One of a fatherless family of nine, he has learned to shoulder heavy responsibilities. Prior to 2002, when he took his final exams, he worked during school holidays in a furniture factory. He was the first of his family to pursue his studies to university level—his father never attended a class in his life, and his older brother never got to high school. His mother would like him to be a doctor and is counting on him to help out his six sisters later on.

Yussef himself would like to get to a foreign country, to study medicine and live out the destiny that his mother has mapped for him. He's a serious boy, the hope of his family. He only smiles when he talks about football. He once dreamed of being part of a World Cup qualifying team. Today he belongs to the Balata soccer club, which used to have matches with teams from other towns before the camp was sealed off by the al-Aqsa Intifada. Their last away game was against a club from

Hebron in the southern West Bank zone. It took Yussef's Balata team several hours to get there because their bus was stopped and thoroughly searched by the IDF.

Palestinian teenagers are condemned to live in a shrunken world. Most have never left the West Bank or the Gaza Strip. Those brought up in the working-class quarters and the refugee camps identify strongly with the place where they live, which they practically never leave. Unlike their elders, they have no contact with Israeli society. Too young to obtain permits authorizing them to sell their labor on the other side of the Green Line, few of their number have ever seen the inside of an Israeli jail.[4] The suspicion engendered by their almost total ignorance of the ways of the other side has hardly inclined these young people to moderation.

Nor is moderation much taught by the official political organizations, because many of these young people declare themselves free of any party affiliation. Whereas the experience of the first Intifada had the effect of structuring activists within the various political formations, those between fifteen and twenty years old at the close of the 1990s escaped participation in the national struggle and the social pressures that went with it. At that time the political movements were putting very little money and energy into recruiting new militants; the parties of the left had been steadily running out of steam for several years; and Hamas, savagely repressed, was in no shape to solicit new members. As for Fatah, the Palestinian Authority was dead against it asserting itself as an independent political force.

Thus the setting up of the Authority had changed the certainties and outlook of an entire population. The battle against the Israeli occupiers had settled the Palestinians' political identity, and the few years of precarious peace that followed had done little to help the younger generation acquire a more partisan identity of its own. The choices made by the Authority raised painful dissension and conflict within society, and all Palestinians were to some extent unsettled by the breakdown of the unanimity that had held so well throughout the first Intifada. The young were even more affected, and the unleashing of a fresh Intifada against Israel did little to clear the political air. Young Palestinians loudly expressed their rejection of the divisions affecting their people, which they thought wrong and negative. Emerging from adolescence, they tended to see the political infighting as totally sterile and foolish; they were violently critical of the politicians for their failure to agree. The leadership's ambiguous attitude toward the activists confused the issue even more. Teenagers particularly resented the powerlessness of the Authority to protect its own population, when they weren't calling in question its will to defend the national cause. "What on earth can our security services do about the Israelis confiscating our land?" complains Yussef. "Write a report? Pay compensation? And how about when they cut down our trees to build their settlements? I think the Authority is just getting weaker and weaker, to the point where people will turn against it for good. I mean, we're being bombed and shot at in our Zone A cities!"

A schoolgirl in Balata thinks this of the members of the Palestinian government: "I believe some of them are working with the Israeli Army, but the others are patriotic, like the sons of our people ought to be."

Nevertheless, whether they're still in school or already working as low-level employees, young Palestinians articulate clear political needs and long for leaders capable of transcending party differences and working out new ways forward. Yussef says he hopes political personalities may still emerge "who can recreate unity and organize military and political training so we really understand what to do next and how to act" because the stone-throwing "no longer serves any purpose at all." Most think that no existing political force is anywhere near up to this role. Like the rest of society—of which they are the magnified reflection[5]—young Palestinians are thoroughly confused by the derailment of Palestinian nationalism and by the drift among its leaders. The idealization of a glorious past, perceived as a time of cohesion and solidarity, makes their anguish even sharper.

Critical as they are of the party political system, fifteen-to-twenty-year-olds remain radically nationalistic, ferocious critics of the state of Israel. Most think Israel should be wiped off the map. The grandchildren of the original refugees talk about their right of return to the villages of their origin. To this position of political intransigence may frequently be added a highly negative perception of Israelis themselves, who are described as "cruel," "racist," and "materialistic." You have to push Yussef quite hard before he will consent to temper these views a little: "I'm sure there are some good Jews who are good people, even if

I've never met any. And Islam protects Christians and Jews alike." But when exactly did Yussef have an opportunity to observe for himself the humanity of Israelis? He remembers the first Intifada and his terror when the soldiers came to search the houses and harass the shebab. He remembers how he wasn't allowed to play soccer when the curfew was in force. During the popular demonstrations in Nablus in March 2001, Yussef saw the effects of an IDF dumdum bullet on one of his friends. "I was right beside him. He slumped against me and drenched me with blood. Bits of his brain were all over the ground."

The older ones are sometimes surprised by the radicalism of their younger brothers, even though several elements unite to nourish this phenomenon. The age gap and their consequent lack of experience are a first explanation. Between the ages of fifteen and twenty, political engagement is often lived out very fully, with ideals determining aspirations and opinions. Inexperience of life and confinement within a cramped social space go a long way toward keeping the younger generation unsullied by pragmatism. Paradoxically, the daily, direct confrontation with Israel tends to bring individuals down to earth, and to make them acknowledge the reality of a neighboring Jewish state with which sooner or later they will have to come to terms. To this is added the context of extreme violence in which today's youth have to live. The Israeli repression, with its bombings and humiliations, its shootings of unarmed or lightly armed demonstrators, is no recipe for moderation. Many of these young people have seen death up close, at first hand. Finally, the effect of Islamist ideology is perfectly visible, even among the sons and daughters of families that support Fatah. Islamism points them toward the dream of a reconquered Palestinian Mandate, in which the Jews would be allowed to live within an Islamic state, tolerated as befits a religious minority. It focuses their imagination on the figure of the martyr. The longing to re-create the unanimity of the first Intifada is grafted on to the Islamist interpretation of today's conflict. The fusion of these two dimensions is clear whenever young Palestinians take on Israeli tanks with nothing but rocks in their hands, and whenever they risk their lives without remotely endangering those of their adversaries. The heroic aspect of these acts links them with the myth of the first Intifada, while the death that threatens is a gauge of martyrdom. Rage, intermingled with a sense of futility, prompts their ultimately useless acts:

to pelt with stones a soldier with an automatic rifle, a helmet, and a bulletproof vest can only put one's own life at risk. Several hundred Palestinian children and teenagers have died in the course of these utterly unequal confrontations.[6] The difficulty they have in formulating personal plans for the future, a future that appears so completely blocked to them, also goes some way to explaining their interest in death.

In Balata, when you ask the younger brothers what they plan to do with their lives, a certain number always say they want to be martyrs. They announce this quite straightforwardly, without bothering to explain whether their action would also mean inflicting damage on the enemy. This attitude reflects the disarray of an entire generation—and through it the disarray of society as a whole, which finds itself powerless to find any way at all of thwarting the Israelis.

Mansur was wounded in the leg during a demonstration in Nablus. "I join in every time I get the chance. It's always throwing stones. So what? The Israelis might kill me any other time I go out in the street." Mansur hopes he will die a martyr one day. But why not think about another kind of future? He won't let himself do that until Palestine is free. "And I don't see that ever happening." It's an effort for Mansur, but after some judicious prodding he does allow his private longings to come to the surface. "If there was a real Palestinian state, I'd like to be a soldier and go back to my studies. Maybe computers, maybe chemistry like Yahya Ayache.[7] I'd like to go and live in my parents' village, Kfar Qassem. Our family house is still there. And if that's not possible I'll stay in Balata. I'd like to travel, though, and see the Eiffel Tower in Paris. But above all I want to live in my own country. Palestine must be an Islamic nation where justice is guaranteed . . . a democracy, like the one in Israel today."

To die, or to study. To die, or to live in the land of one's ancestors. Faced with the constraints of the occupation, which smother every form of social, economic, or personal aspiration, Palestinian youth are caught between the impossibility of living under such circumstances and the dream of effacing the exile of their kin. It seems to them absolutely necessary to send in more and more suicide bombers, if Palestine is ever to be liberated. All the volunteers who blow themselves up in the heart of Israel's cities are recruited from a group between eighteen and twenty-four years old.

Mansur is no supporter of Hamas, but he points out that the way they operate is the only thing that can tilt the balance of power away from the Israelis. Yussef roughly agrees with this. He would be ready to take up arms himself, but under the present circumstances he sees little point in doing so. The suicide bombers are the only ones who are actually, physically striking a target.

These random bombings against Israeli civilians have provoked the fury of westerners, who cannot comprehend them. They are also denounced by a sizable number of Palestinian intellectuals as a fundamentally illegitimate means of furthering a political aim. Beyond this moral condemnation, public opinion appears to be staggered by the apparently irrational nature of the act, committed as it always is by extremely young people who decide to turn themselves into human bombs. Some people believe that the suicide bombers are the victims of cynical, manipulative political leaders who use hideous methods to train them as killing machines. Others consider the suicide attack the ultimate expression of Palestinian despair. These approaches are oversimplified and fail to take account of the political, social, and psychological mechanisms that underlie the suicide bombing just as they ignore the breadth of the phenomenon, which has gained more and more momentum and many new protagonists. To explain the bombings is not to decipher the logic that underscores this tilt toward radical violence.

Those who carry out suicide attacks claim that in doing so they can diminish and even reverse the overwhelming advantage held by the Israeli Army over the Palestinian fighters. Their aim is to overcome the latter's inability to make effective use of legitimate violence, and to direct them toward a much more radical use of it. The organization of a suicide attack requires few materials or human resources; it merely needs know-how and a certain imagination to elude the vigilance of Israeli soldiers and police, as well as careful preparation involving a restricted number of people. Its success basically depends on the determination of its author and mastery of the technical and psychological skills involved in the process. These range from the acquisition of explosives to the illegal crossing of the Green Line, the adoption of a way of behaving and holding oneself that will hoodwink the Israelis, and choice of the correct timing and the best target for the final detonation. As a tactic, the suicide bombing offers Palestinian fighters something they would never obtain by the use of classic guerrilla warfare procedures—namely, significant physical losses inflicted on the enemy and a deep psychological impact on his mind. The brutal rationale of the suicide bomber's act is that of destabilizing the adversary.

Islamist rhetoric explains the vulnerability of Israeli society by the fact that its members are afraid of death. Their argument consists in demonstrating that Israeli soldiers, despite their ultrasophisticated equipment, are no match for Palestinians person for person. Believing that the Achilles heel of the Israelis lies in their attachment to life, the men of *Jihad* look beyond their own obvious inferiority in terms of weaponry. They calculate that their willingness to sacrifice themselves gives them a moral superiority over the citizens of the Israeli state. Giving their lives in the battle against Israel is an option that all Palestinian militants (whether Islamists or otherwise) look upon with a certain fatalism. They know that they are in a situation of inferiority, and they evaluate the risks they run with simple pragmatism. Overriding all this is a traditional concept of society, which affirms the preeminence of the interests of the community over those of the individual. Both the organizers and the authors of suicide attacks see Israel as a fundamentally hedonistic, materialistic society with lapsed moral and religious values. Consequently the radical activists seek to terrorize the Israelis by indiscriminate killing and maiming. Their hope is that fear will lead the Israeli government to buckle, and/or that a significant number of Israeli citizens will simply leave the country. The plan, in short, is to terrorize the Israelis by repeatedly targeting their point of greatest weakness.

A spirit of revenge, and a desire to slaughter the adversary, also have their place among the suicide bomber's motivations, since most of the attacks are presented as ripostes to the killing of Palestinian civilians in the course of IDF operations within the Territories, or as vengeance for the killing of political or military leaders. With symmetrical promptness, the Israeli authorities launch their own reprisals with the stated intention of eradicating "nests of terrorists."

The recourse to terrorist violence clearly demonstrates that there has been not only a drastic reduction in the means available to carry on the struggle against Israeli occupation, but also a growing incapacity on the part of Palestinian society to come up with new approaches to the fight. The impossibility of doing anything significant and a feeling of utter futility are articulated by young people everywhere, indeed by the Palestinian population in general. Although the principle of struggle against the Israeli state enjoys their full support, they seriously doubt the effectiveness of the operations conducted by the shebab. Paradoxically, their very real and deeply felt impotence vis-à-vis Israel leads some of them to embrace the idea of total violence. On an individual level, the young must grapple with their incapacity to make plans for any kind of future, or to build their lives like their contemporaries in other countries. Their prospects for further education or for earning a living are fraught with uncertainty, dogged by financial constraints, and painfully hampered by the restrictions on their movement within the Palestinian Territories and abroad. The sheer difficulty of fulfilling oneself personally under such circumstances is bound to restrict any dispositions one might make in terms of love, marriage, or raising a family. Not only does the Israeli repression have a real practical effect on the daily lives of people in the West Bank and Gaza, it also affects their mental outlook in a very profound way. The sense of being relieved of any real choice with respect to their own existence is one that the shebab often express; hence the meticulous arrangement of their own demise, in the act of striking at the heart of enemy society, paradoxically allows them to regain control of their lives—if only at the last moment—and in doing so to inflict upon the enemy a devastating revenge for what he has done to them. They can escape the iron ring of impotence to which both they and their community are shackled, by choosing the way of the martyred hero. The reverberations that can be expected in terms of human losses, their likely psychological impact, and the posthumous prestige to be expected by the martyr are also among the desirable consequences anticipated in the suicide attack.

For the Islamists of Hamas and Islamic Jihad, the carrying out of a suicide attack also has a religious dimension, born of the certainty of accomplishing a duty and the prospect of bliss in the afterlife. Ideological training and insertion into a militant network are decisive in this case.

The leaders of the Islamist movements insist that candidates for martyrdom go through a religious preparation. The suicide bomber only receives instructions to act when the guides feel that the bomber's faith is sufficiently strong to allow success in the mission. A communiqué signed by one Hamas bomber shows how firmly he and his like feel themselves justified by their religion:

> Our meeting with God is better and more precious than this life. I swear by the same God that in another place there is a paradise wider than the firmament above the earth, for life today is no more than a diversion, a distraction, and a search for wealth. . . . An operation on behalf of Jihad, carried out by a fighter whose heart is filled with belief and love of his country, strikes terror into the hearts of the arrogant and makes them tremble.[8]

Immediately following the 1993 peace accords with Israel, the Palestinian Islamists denounced the treachery of their people's negotiators and called for an all-out Jihad. Thereafter, concluding that the Palestinian Authority is powerless either to protect its citizens against the machinations of the Israeli secret service or to complete the national design, Hamas has claimed to be the embodiment of devotion to the nation and of duty to Islam. With the outbreak of the al-Aqsa Intifada, the Islamists again set about organizing suicide attacks.

A turning point was reached in early 2002 when the al-Aqsa Martyrs Brigade, an armed group claiming affiliation with Fatah and formed to fight in the new Intifada, adopted the methods of the Islamists by carrying out a series of suicide bombings against Israeli civilians. In this way they diverged from the line taken by their nominal leaders, who had declared certain limits to the conflict. For example, the Fatah leadership had specified that only soldiers and settlers present in the West Bank and Gaza were legitimate targets. In reaction to a vigorous Israeli campaign of repression, Fatah's base became radicalized and began to defy the directives of its leaders. The resultant proliferation of attacks was part of a simple process of demand and supply within the framework of nationalist mobilization. Fatah's military wing began recruiting girls as well as young men, and this also led to innovations in technique. Given the ever more ferocious methods of the Israeli Army, the balance of power between the two sides became even more unequal, and so the present use of extreme violence by both is now aimed at nothing less than forcing the enemy to cease using the weapons of greatest advantage.

All these factors have combined to encourage the generation of younger brothers—and younger sisters—to sacrifice themselves as human bombs. Unlike their elders, they have no real political culture, and they want nothing to do with the traditional party structures. To be a suicide bomber, on the other hand, is to short-circuit sterile politics, to transcend the collective defeat of the Palestinian people, and to strike a heavy individual blow against the enemy.

The change wrought by pressure from the radicals seems itself to have sprung from a deliberate tactical choice. Although the new kamikazes are less concerned with religion than one might expect, this development demonstrates beyond any shadow of doubt that Palestinian society is gradually becoming Islamized. Hamas has not won any notable political victories since the beginning of the al-Aqsa Intifada, but still it has succeeded in spreading its ideology by setting up the martyr-figure as the definitive model for Palestinian struggle. During the first months of the al-Aqsa Intifada, the stone-throwers could fill this role by falling before the guns of the Israeli soldiery. Now, as the deadly cycle of violence and reprisal steadily accelerates, there is an unmistakable will to replace the victim-martyr with the hero-martyr.

AN ORDINARY FRIDAY IN RAMALLAH

A demonstration, which has become a ritual, takes place in Ramallah each Friday. After the prayer-hour, a few hundred individuals carrying Palestinian flags and the banners of the various political parties assemble at the main intersection at the center of town. From here they march to Betil, the Israeli military camp a few kilometers from the twin locality of al-Bireh. The procession stops a few meters from a line of Israeli Army jeeps, some of the young people hurl stones at the vehicles, the soldiers reply with tear gas and rubber bullets, and the demonstrators disperse.

On one notable occasion, the situation degenerated.

Katia, a Canadian journalist, was covering the event one Friday. When the crowd fled for cover, she stayed where she was, more or less protected from the IDF bullets by a concrete pylon. She wasn't scared, thinking that her photographic reporter's paraphernalia would serve to protect her since the soldiers were quite close enough to make them out. The square was empty when suddenly she became disagreeably aware that an Israeli sniper was concentrating his fire on her. She ran for it but took a bullet in the calf of her leg and fell in the open. Two young Palestinians scrambled to help her, alone in the face of the soldiers; at the time there were no stones flying and no bullets coming from the Palestinian side. An ambulance appeared, but the sniper kept up a steady fire. One of the shebab helping Katia was hit full in the head. He died a few hours later in the same hospital as the young journalist he had been assisting.[9] While this drama was unfolding, armed shebab were waiting patiently at a crossroads several hundred yards back from the area of confrontation. No Palestinian civilian had been authorized to remain within the perimeter separating them from the IDF. One group had taken up its position in a street leading to the area where the demonstration had taken place; its members were hidden behind an empty house at the top of the slope. In this zone, a few Palestinian families had evacuated because of the danger of bullets spattering the front of their houses. The rest, mostly because they were too poor to afford the move, had remained where they were.

The shebab, bristling with cell phones and M16 rifles, had arrived by car. Posted at the top of the street, they were awaiting orders from their chief, Hussein Sheikh, a Fatah leader aged about forty. Sheikh is on record as saying that if the Israelis sincerely wanted peace, he would be ready to send his own son up to the Green Line as a guarantee that Israeli lives would be protected. Now, however, he considered that the level of Israeli provocation demanded that the Intifada be resumed, and he had reassembled a group of young men aged about twenty who were loyal to him. Although they all had jobs in the Palestinian security services, they had given them up to join the battle against the Israelis.

The shebab crawled around and loosed off their rifles, but the Israeli troops stayed perfectly safe behind their fortifications. This did not prevent the sheikh's protégés from behaving like cowboys: to show their courage and virility, they refused to don the bulletproof vests that had been issued to them. The Fatah representative followed the course the battle via his mobile phone. Soon he was dancing with rage at the news that his men had moved down to another position, held by a different group, behind a building that served as a vantatge point. The resump-

tion of hostilities had not by any means wiped away the rivalries between the various groups.

Actually it now appears that Yasser Arafat's political formation in
Ramallah was, and remains, riven with dissension. Hussein Sheikh and
Marwan Barghuti both claimed the title of Fatah chief in the West
Bank. As rival candidates in the Fatah leadership elections, they were
unable to settle the issue because the last round of balloting never took
place, leaving several delegates in dispute. During this difficult period,
Yasser Arafat was unwilling to allow a completed process to decide between two rivals who snubbed and disliked one another, despite having
many points of agreement. Marwan Barghuti was a star performer on
al-Jazeera and a number of other TV stations; banished from the Territories by the Israelis prior to the first Intifada, he had taken part in its
direction from Amman and then, in 1996, had been elected to the Legislative Council as a member of Fatah. Sheikh also belonged to a generation of men who were in the forefront of the 1987 rising. A fervent
supporter of the Oslo accords, he was all for the principle of peace in exchange for security and territory in exchange for a Palestinian pledge
not to attack Israeli civilians. Furthermore, he supported the policy of
repressing the Islamists and had participated in the setting up of the
Preventive Security Force before being removed from its inner circle of
leaders.

But when it came to fighting, none of these distinctions mattered a
jot to the IDF troops, who in the late afternoon launched three rocket-
propelled grenades at their tormentors, to bring the action to an end.
The shebab were clustered together in one place. There were three ex-
plosions, and three Palestinians were carried away injured.

All this time, a couple named Amal and Khalil and their two
daughters were sitting huddled at the far end of their apartment, waiting for the shooting to stop. The windows shook with the detonations;
the couple's older child, a girl aged five, stayed calm enough, but their
three-year-old shrieked with terror all afternoon. Amal was cool, Khalil
less so. Stuck in a building under constant small arms fire, the young
couple grumbled about the unending cycle of confrontation. "It's serving no purpose whatever," was Khalil's conclusion. "Sooner or later
they'll start negotiating again." Finally, at nightfall, their ordeal came to
an end. The family tried to decompress with a sortie to the square, in the

upper part of Ramallah. The parents sat and smoked while the children played on the swings.

Originally, since there was no telling how long the fighting would last, Amal and Khalil had decided to move out of a building they had been occupying on a temporary basis. They had some money set aside, and with this and a twenty-year mortgage they bought an apartment in a new luxury block in al-Bireh. In November 2001 the family's possessions were boxed up and moved; simultaneously—unfortunately for them—Israeli tanks were sent in to reoccupy certain zones under Palestinian sovereignty, in particular the environs of Yasser Arafat's headquarters and a part of al-Bireh. The brand new building in which Amal and Khalil planned to live was still empty; the IDF troops took advantage of this to occupy it and ransack the interiors of the apartments. The floors were quickly smeared with filth, and the kitchens and bathrooms smashed up. So not unnaturally the couple postponed moving in themselves.

At the same time the premises of the Palestinian Central Bureau of Statistics[10] were wrecked. The organization's computers were smashed or confiscated by the Israelis. Since the bureau was close to Amal and Khalil's apartment, they had to wait for the Israeli Army to evacuate the building before they could start repairs. They did, however, obtain some funds toward doing this from the Palestinian Authority, the balance being made up from their own pockets. But when they finally arrived in their new home, they found they had an uninterrupted view of the massed tanks of the Israeli Army.

Amal, Khalil, and their daughters were routinely obliged to stay inside after sundown. The zone was too dangerous during the hours of darkness. It was difficult, even impossible, for them to sleep. In reprisal for suicide bombings, the Israelis bombed Gaza and Ramallah at the end of 2001. The family passed many a sleepless night at that time.

They were also plagued with money worries, day after day. Their younger daughter nominally attended the nursery, which—when it wasn't subject to the Israeli curfew—was constantly having to close its doors for safety reasons, forcing Amal to take the child to work with her. Khalil ran a print shop with his brother, and Amal, an imaginative and energetic businesswoman, had set up an advertising agency two years earlier. But since the reoccupation of part of the town, some of her agency's clients had gone bankrupt while others had drastically reduced their advertising budgets.

By mid-2002 Amal found herself with only 10 percent of her normal turnover, which in turn obliged her to lay off four of her seven employees. Nor was she sure of paying the rent for her offices each month, since there was no question of their owner giving her any kind of credit. In the modern complex he had built, intended for prestige firms, only ten offices remained occupied out of a total of more than sixty.

Though they live in Ramallah, Amal and Khalil are both from Nablus: for the feast of Aid, they are in the habit of driving home to visit their parents. This year, for the second year running, they aren't going. Their hometown may be only fifty kilometers away, but Israeli Army roadblocks lengthen the journey by many hours. To take their own car is highly risky, because the Israeli soldiers often force passengers out, make the driver park on the shoulder, and confiscate the keys. And even if one manages to stay at the wheel of the car, one still has to find one's own way, taking tracks across country, because the main roads have been rendered impassable by the IDF. Even to go in a collective taxi is far from safe, since these too must run the gauntlet of humiliating searches by Israeli conscripts along the way.

OPERATION PICTURESQUE JOURNEY

On Thursday, February 28, 2002, the Israeli Army launched an assault on two West Bank refugee camps, Jenin and Balata. The code name for the operation was Picturesque Journey, chosen at random by a computer and confirmed by the general staff. The reoccupation of Zone A, which had been under Palestinian civil and military control, had begun in May 2000 with the overrunning by the IDF of a village in northern Gaza that lasted for several hours. After that, the same pattern was repeated on a number of occasions, but the February 2002 attack on the camps was unprecedented and signaled a major escalation in the intensity of the repression. The Israeli objective was to arrest activists and seize guns and explosives, while demonstrating that there was nowhere for the Palestinian fighters to hide—the IDF could strike when and where it wished. The raid was carried out in reprisal for a series of attacks against military targets and settlers in the West Bank, and against civilians within Israel.

Since the beginning of 2002, the armed shebab had acquired a number of new combat skills. Some groups had mastered entirely different guerrilla techniques, and they managed to inflict significant losses on the enemy. The al-Aqsa Intifada appeared to have reached a turning point.

In the afternoon of that Thursday, Israeli tanks massed around Balata, completing its encirclement. The generator that provided the camp's electricity was knocked out, plunging the inhabitants into darkness. The soldiers ordered everyone to come out of their houses and leave. An overwhelming majority refused to do so and defied the threats: the refugees remembered only too well what leaving cost them in 1948, and they had no intention of risking their homes a second time. Meanwhile, the Intifada militants among them managed to slip away to a safe haven outside the camp.

At six o'clock in the evening, an IDF special unit burst into Iman's house. Her brother, a Fatah political representative, was out inquiring about the people who had been hurt and Iman was at home with her elderly mother, her brother's small children, and her sister-in-law, who was seven months pregnant. The soldiers demanded that they give up their menfolk along with their weapons. Iman replied that there were no weapons on the premises and nobody was in the house but women and children. The troops could look wherever they wanted, she added, holding out the keys to her brother's apartment on the floor above. Ignoring this, they forced Iman out of the way and when she resisted lashed her wrists and locked her in a tiny bedroom along with the rest of the family. Iman's mother took out her Koran and began to read; the sister-in-law passed out cold, and the two children, aged six and eight, burst out screaming and crying. Shams, the four-year-old boy, was petrified into a profound silence that lasted till the following day. For twenty-four hours no one was allowed out, either to eat or to relieve themselves. Iman's mother, a diabetic, was in dire need of medication, but their jailors were implacable. At intervals throughout the night a soldier opened the door and checked with a torch that nothing subversive was going on. Finally, late on Friday afternoon, Iman and her family were permitted to go to their kitchen and bathroom for a few minutes. Iman gave her nephews some bread, olive oil, and dried thyme—all the other food had spoiled in the refrigerator because of the power cut. A soldier presented himself as a military doctor and told her he could treat the children if necessary. "The children are all right for the moment," Iman replied. "But if you really have their interests at heart, you'll just leave us alone." The soldier's eyes seemed to suggest that none of this was any of his doing, and he turned away.

One of his comrades tore a framed photo from the wall above Iman's bed. It was a snapshot of Sami, posing with his gun shortly before the day of his death.

"Who's this?"

"My fiancé. Your army killed him."

"A terrorist. So you go with terrorists?"

"He wasn't a terrorist. He was a resistance fighter. He died a martyr."

"So he's dead. Where's his gun? You know where it is."

"I haven't a clue where it is. We didn't live together. How should I know about things like that?"

The soldier ripped the snapshot out of its frame, tore it to pieces, and ground them into the floor with the heel of his boot. Iman waited for him to finish, then stooped to gather the shredded image of the man she had loved.

The twenty or so soldiers occupying the house had soiled the family's living room with cigarette butts, and all the rooms had been ransacked. While Iman was feeding Shams, she realized the child was terrified, hunched up and avoiding the eyes of the soldiers. The "martyr's" fiancée spoke to him sternly: "Raise your head and look these men in the eye. There's no need to be scared. They're not monsters—they're people just like us, with arms, legs, eyes, and a mouth. Meet their eyes, look at them straight!"

Shams hesitated, then shot the soldiers a brief, shy glance.

That Sunday, in the late morning, the siege of Balata was finally over. The soldiers went away, leaving the family's two apartments—among many others—totally wrecked. The door on the second floor, whose key Iman had offered, was smashed to pieces. The TV and the VCR were broken, the mattresses had been eviscerated, the wardrobes emptied, the schoolbooks and the Palestinian passports ripped to shreds.

The Israeli operation against the refugee camps of Balata and Jenin resulted in a death toll of twenty-one people—nineteen Palestinians, including an eight-year-old girl, and two Israeli soldiers. Over two hundred Palestinians were injured as the army rampaged through house after house, blasting their way through walls to avoid exposing themselves to the bullets of Palestinian fighters in the open street. "The camps were supposed to be invulnerable, but the lion turned out to be a rabbit," exulted Yitzhak Eytan, the commander of the central region.[11]

Despite the heavy loss of life, it would appear that on this occasion the IDF fell well short of its objectives in terms of flushing out activists and seizing weapons. On the other hand, angry new recruits flocked to the militant cause, and suicide bombings increased dramatically. On Saturday, March 2, a suicide attack killed nine people in West Jerusalem; on Sunday, a Palestinian sniper with a gun dating from the Second World War shot dead seven Israeli soldiers and three settlers at a roadblock north of Ramallah; on Monday, a Palestinian man blew himself up in a bus at Afula and another killed three people in Tel Aviv. Numerous rockets were fired at Israeli cities from the Gaza Strip. And of course the Israelis hit back with reprisals. An eye for an eye, a tooth for a tooth: the process continued inexorably.

THE VICIOUS CIRCLE

In April 2002 the Israeli Army tackled the mission of finally eradicating all sources of Palestinian terrorism. It mounted a major, unprecedented operation that touched several Palestinian towns and was especially aimed at the refugee camp at Jenin and the old town of Nablus.

The Jenin refugee camp with its fifteen thousand souls was viewed as a nest of suicide bombers by the Israeli authorities.[12] The attack on

Jenin was unusually ferocious; it caused widespread indignation among the international community and sowed doubt in many Israeli circles.

On April 3, tanks surrounded the camp and a curfew was declared. Some of the inhabitants managed to get away to neighboring villages, but the majority went to ground in their own homes. Shellfire and helicopter missiles rained down on the camp. To make the roads passable for the army's vehicles and more secure for infantry units, bulldozers leveled swathes of buildings beside the road. The offices of the Palestinian Authority were systematically targeted. Palestinian fighters, entrenched and lightly armed, gave battle to the intruders. Despite their inferiority in numbers and equipment, they succeeded in drawing the Israelis into a trap, in which thirteen troops were killed. To avert even greater losses, the IDF hardened its tactics. Scores of houses were dynamited or flattened. Homes were brutally and systematically turned upside down, and families were herded into one room of their homes while the soldiers searched, inspected, and looted jewelry and other valuables. Men were requisitioned to serve as human shields for IDF units as they broke into houses. The Israeli military shot to kill at anyone who dared to break the curfew. Guided in by spotters on the ground, missiles were launched at targets considered to present a danger. These surgical strikes reduced but did not eliminate civilian casualties. After a few days of savage fighting, the last Palestinian guns fell silent.

Estimates of the death toll among the Palestinians of Jenin varied between fifty-four and two hundred, but in fact the entombment of both living and dead under the ruins of the collapsed buildings made any kind of reliable final count impossible. Twenty-three Israeli soldiers were killed and sixty wounded in the fighting. Some parts of the Jenin camp were completely destroyed, and by April 17 when the siege was lifted there were at least four thousand homeless.

The entire zone was sealed off for the duration of the operation; no foreign or Israeli journalist was allowed to approach it for as long as the operation lasted. Humanitarian organizations were not authorized to enter the camp and consequently were unable to treat the injured. Amnesty International published a report in November 2002 in which it was flatly stated that certain acts committed by the Israeli Army at Jenin and Nablus were classifiable war crimes. The report provides a detailed breakdown of illegal homicides, instances of the use of Palestinians as human shields, obstruction of medical and humanitarian assistance, deliberate demolition of buildings, and wanton destruction of property.

Part of the old town of Nablus was destroyed. The bulldozers of the Israeli Army made no exception for buildings of historical importance: the al-Khudra Mosque, one of the most ancient Muslim places of worship in the world, was severely damaged. The Israeli objective was to reduce to nothing the outposts held by any Palestinians still inclined to offer a fight. Between March 29 and April 22, more than eighty Palestinians were killed, including seven women and nine children. Najy and Bassam both escaped.

In the West Bank as a whole, the IDF conducted a mass roundup of males in the towns and refugee camps. Six thousand men,[13] ordinary civilians along with militants, found themselves in makeshift detention centers without adequate shelter or food where they were subjected to all manner of ill-treatment. Their conditions were all the more dire in that the Israeli Army had nothing like the material resources required to hold thousands of prisoners. Two-thirds of the detainees were freed after a few days or weeks. Some were turned loose in their hometown centers, where they were immediately pulled in again by Israeli patrols enforcing the curfew.

In June 2002 another suicide attack took place in Jerusalem. In reprisal, the IDF launched Operation Road Closed which resulted in the long-term reoccupation of all the towns of the West Bank except Jericho. This operation over a much wider area was carried out less summarily than those that had gone before, but its more lasting nature had the effect of finishing off what remained of the economic fabric and political organization of Palestinian society.

Nablus and the refugee camps around it were kept under curfew for three months. Nobody was allowed to his or her place of work, the schools were closed, and life came to a dead halt within the walls of overcrowded buildings. Every two or three days, families were allowed to go out for a few hours to buy food. Shopkeepers wrestled with severe difficulties in maintaining stocks. The functionaries of the Palestinian Authority continued to receive their stipends, but the private sector had to lay off workers in droves. Many households saw their last savings melt away completely. Access to medical care was awkward and uncertain. The precedence given to people needing emergency medical attention became purely theoretical, because checks on ambulances by Israeli soldiers could last for several hours at a time.

The West Bank was transformed into about three hundred small enclaves, each isolated from the next. Most roads were placed out of bounds to Palestinian vehicles, in the interest of greater security. The IDF made many impassable by digging trenches across them. A few collective taxis did their best to link the districts via dirt tracks and lengthy detours, but even so they were subjected to rigorous army searches. Donkeys and mules reappeared as forms of transport. Unlike the owners of cars, at least people with beasts of burden ran no risk that their property would be confiscated. The villages that depended on neighboring urban concentrations for basic supplies were particularly hard hit. On several occasions Beit Furik, a tiny village a few miles from Nablus, found itself without water for weeks on end. Those there who lived by farming the land were hit very hard; hundreds of their olive trees were simply flattened. When at last the raising of the curfew allowed them to return to their fields, the villagers found themselves under attack from Jewish settlers installed nearby. The bullets and flying stones duly had their effect. There was no olive harvest in the West Bank in 2002.

In the course of Operation Road Closed, Bassam was finally caught by the IDF and sent to a prison in Israel. Najy found himself the last free survivor of the original Balata group. He went underground yet again, and even when the curfew was finally lifted in early October he never showed himself in the open unless it was to move to a safer hideout. In mortal fear of electronic eavesdropping, he juggled the mobile phones through which he issued his instructions to the remaining cells of al-Aqsa Martyrs. One year after the death of his friend Sami, he tried to convince Iman to marry Bassam, the group's last bachelor. Despite his insistence and the arguments he brought to bear, Iman firmly refused the match.

The Israeli Army's occupation and repression of the Palestinian Territories did not prevent another surge of suicide bombings. Notwithstanding the blockades, the curfews, the arrests, and the surgical assassinations, Palestinian attacks continued uninterrupted. The result was that the wisdom and effectiveness of the Israeli strategy began to be called in question. On July 17, 2002, a man blew himself up in Tel Aviv.

Two weeks later, the father of a family planted a bomb in the cafeteria of Jerusalem's Hebrew University. More deadly bombs went off on August 4 and September 18. On November 11, there was a shocking incident involving the small community living at the Metzer Kibbutz, in which a member of Fatah's military wing murdered five people, including a woman and her two children. Ten days later, an attack by Hamas inside Jerusalem killed eleven people and led to the reoccupation of Bethlehem.

December 2002 was relatively calm. But just before the feast of Aid, Najy was at last intercepted by Israeli forces. After a month's interrogation, he was sent to a prison in the south of Israel. Like the other inmates, he was barred from receiving visitors before his trial. A report by an Israeli human rights organization published in January 2003 indicates that Israel was detaining more than a thousand Palestinians without trial at that time.

And yet Israeli daily life has continued to be plagued by regular acts of terror. On January 5, 2003, a double attack claimed by several different Palestinian organizations killed twenty-three people in Tel Aviv, plunging the nation into anguish three weeks prior to the general election. On March 5 the suicide bombing of a bus in Haifa killed fifteen more Israelis.

The authorities are persisting with their campaign of raids and incursions into Palestinian territory. Two months after taking up his command, the new Israeli chief of staff, General Moshe Yaalon, made this comment: "The Palestinian threat is perfectly invisible. It's like a cancer . . . if you fail to diagnose it correctly and people say it's not a cancer, only a headache, the treatment won't work. I think it's a cancer. There are all kinds of treatments for the symptoms of cancer. Some say you should cut out the diseased organs altogether. For the time being, I'm applying chemotherapy."[14]

CONCLUSION

Between the abortive attempts of the international community to impose a ceasefire between the IDF and the Palestinians and the outbreak of the second gulf war on March 20, 2003, the peace proposal of Prince Abdallah of Saudi Arabia suggesting the normalization of Arab relations with Israel in exchange for its withdrawal from all the territories occupied since 1967 has been overtaken by the logic of war. Approved by the participants in the Arab League summit in March 2002, the Saudi proposal and the perspective of a regional settlement seemed unrealistic at the time given the daily death toll in the Palestinian Territories and in Israel. By March 2003, one year later, 2,789 people had been killed since the outbreak of the al-Aqsa Intifada on September 28, 2000: 1,890 Palestinians and 899 Israelis. The intervening twenty-four months of confrontation had proved bloodier than the seven years of the first rising put together.[1]

The Israeli repression has grown enormously in intensity. The IDF has done its worst to crush the Palestinian revolt and continues to deploy unprecedented means to finish the job. Israel's stranglehold on the West Bank and the Gaza Strip and its reoccupation of part of the autonomous Territories has paralyzed the movement of Palestinian people and goods within the Territories and the world outside them. Systematic blockades have undermined an already fragile economy and have hugely restricted Palestinian access to schools, universities, jobs, and medical care. A growing number of families have absolutely no income whatsoever, and malnutrition is spreading. Posted at the barriers that cut across the West Bank and Gaza, or in the course of their raids, the soldiers have often shown brutality and a deliberate intent to humiliate the Palestinians. The wholesale destruction of Palestinian homes in the refugee camps close to the flashpoints of conflict has plunged their inhabitants into confusion and poverty. Unarmed demonstrators have been fired upon with real bullets, surgical bombings have been carried out in the crowded centers of Palestinian towns, and Fatah and Hamas activists have been ruthlessly eliminated, along with their comrades in other political formations. These tactics, along with raids into the autonomous zones and forays into specific towns, villages, and refugee camps, have been costly in both civilian and military lives. On March 5, 2002, after a particularly bloody week, Ariel Sharon declared that the Palestinians would "have to be hit very hard" because "unless they understand they are beaten, we can never return to the negotiating table."[2] By intensifying their strikes, the Israeli authorities aim to exhaust Palestinian society and dry up its potential for mobilization. Nevertheless, there is no certainty that this strategy can work in the short term. In the long term, it seems to be leading to a complete impasse in the sense that it prevents Israel from building any kind of political project for the future. The Palestinian question cannot, in other words, be solved purely by treating it as a security issue.

For the Israeli repression has led to a serious escalation of violence. Palestinian suicide attacks within Israel continue on a regular basis. The shebab have managed to carry out successful attacks on Jewish soldiers and settlers within the Territories. The Israeli repression has also encouraged extremist elements within the Palestinian populace. In this regard, the conversion of the armed wing of Fatah to Islamist methods, which consist of perpetuating suicide attacks within Israel, is highly significant: it signals a turning point for this group, which formerly followed the path of political pragmatism and favored a secular society. Quite apart from the political changes within the movement, this development reflects an ominous process of radicalization at work within Palestinian society as a whole.

Actually the calculation made by certain Palestinians is nearly identical to that of Sharon himself: to kill as many Israelis as possible would seem to them the only way of making the Israeli state agree to the necessary concessions. The strategy is to work on the sheer lassitude and exasperation of Israeli society, vis-à-vis the moral and human cost of keeping up the occupation of the West Bank and the Gaza Strip. Hezbollah's operation in South Lebanon is seen as an object lesson. This reasoning is far from unrealistic: the protest movement among Israeli army reservists who refuse to serve in the Occupied Territories and the mobilization of Israeli mothers have shown quite clearly that growing numbers of Israelis are no longer willing to pay the price of war. Nevertheless, the impact of the Palestinians' strategy of terrorism has been to strengthen the Israeli people's cohesion around their leaders. The re-election of Ariel Sharon as prime minister in January 2003, the good showing made by Likud and the radical right in the Knesset, and the general collapse of the Israeli Left show that most people support and endorse the former general's security policy. Palestinian violence serves to nourish the bellicose rhetoric that underpins the IDF's tactics of repression.

Thus from the point of view of both protagonists, violence remains the strategy that yields most results: it alone holds out the possibility of a result, insofar as its goal is to compel the enemy to give up.

But both societies will pay a very high price. Significant numbers of Israelis have begun to leave the country, tired of the endless insecurity and the pervasive sense of gloom. In general these people belong to the economic and intellectual elite, people with the economic and cultural resources to start anew in Europe or America. A minister in Ariel Sharon's government has deplored the growing tendency of the children of members of the political class to emigrate. This steady leakage of talent is quietly altering the very nature of Israeli society, whose liberal elements are withering away to the advantage of the religious and nationalist constituency. Divisions are growing. The refusal of about fifty reservist officers and soldiers—known as the *refuzeniks*—to continue serving in the Israeli Army is clear evidence of incipient malaise. The *refuzenik* petition of February 2002 criticized the drift in Israeli military and security matters and asserted the signatories' determination not to participate any further in the "oppression, expulsion, starvation, and humiliation of an entire people," or to "commit war crimes." This initiative broke with the traditional consensus surrounding the IDF and the traditional ideology of the "nation under arms." It gave promise of a real political stand against the occupation. While the idea still has a certain momentum today, it may face stiff opposition from the radical Right, which supports the option of Greater Israel with armed settlers positioned throughout the West Bank and the Gaza Strip. The worsening conflict has hit the Israeli economy very hard, and finally the country is paying a heavy price in terms of international isolation and the tarnishing of its image.

On the Palestinian side, the continuation of the conflict is affecting the cohesion of society, weakening the political system on which it depends, and gradually breaking up the Territories. The ceaseless confrontations are imperiling national solidarity, in the sense that the interests of the middle classes and the armed shebab are ever more divergent. The former attempt to preserve the conditions of their own economic survival; the latter believe that they have nothing to lose and so are prepared to take daring action. Traditional bourgeois families and those with links to the Palestinian Authority continue to hold aloof from the movement, for fear of its political and social consequences. The political edifice built up by the Palestinian leaders of recent years looks exceedingly fragile today. The Islamist movement is no longer kept under control by Yasser Arafat. As for Fatah's militants, some of these have begun to flout the orders of their leaders. The links between the leadership and the grassroots are still intact; the two still work together, but not as closely as they did before. The political class and the representatives of civil society have been overwhelmed. Some politicians and intellectuals favor the tried and tested civil disobedience of the first Intifada, which they feel yielded more benefits. As they see it, the armed struggle has so far served only to keep the Palestinians pinned to a position of hopeless inferiority. But no new tactic for mobilizing civil society has been devised or imposed by these individuals. The weakening of the Palestinian entity is also evident in the diminished ability of its leaders to control the territories over which they are supposed to exercise sovereignty. Regions like the northern West Bank or the southern Gaza Strip, to which officials of the Palestinian Authority can no longer physically go, now tend to organize themselves on an autonomous basis around local warlords. The Israeli repression has considerably enfeebled the capacity of Palestinians to preserve the contours of their political community and create a viable state.

Thus the future of the Israeli-Palestinian conflict looks paradoxical at the very least. In a sense, one might bet on the irresistible tide of history flooding forward to the political emancipation of the Palestinians, whose national destiny is a fact that must be faced sooner or later. And yet in the medium term Palestinian access to full sovereignty within the 1967 boundaries appears unthinkable, blocked as it is by Israeli policy and hampered by an international situation that is most unfavorable to the PLO and the nation it represents. More fundamental choices are at stake, regarding the very nature of the state. If Ariel Sharon can entertain, as he says he does, the idea of forming an authentic Palestinian state, he is nonetheless determined to drain the principle of Palestinian sovereignty of all its meaning. The territorial strategy applied to the West Bank and East Jerusalem reveals a will to conquer and control. In the Holy City, the plan consists in adding three large blocks of settlements to Greater Jerusalem, which is already three times larger on its east side than the pre-1967 Israeli capital. The objective is to build up a belt of settlements so as to cut the town off even further and more definitively from the rest of the West Bank.[3]

The construction of a wall dividing the Arab and Jewish zones would diminish even more the space allotted to the Palestinians. This was designed to guarantee Israeli security while containing the Palestinians behind an impenetrable barrier, bristling with technology to detect the slightest untoward movement. In function of the sites of Israeli settlements scattered over the West Bank, the line of the new frontier would run inside the present Green Line, to the detriment of the Palestinians. Many farmers would be deprived of access to their land, which would henceforward be on the far side of the wall. Likewise a number of Palestinian villages would also be severed from the rest of the West Bank and annexed to the Jewish state. The Israeli state has been practicing, and continues to practice, a policy of fait accompli, whose results it fully intends to make irreversible. Thus if any form of Palestinian state entity were to see the light in the mid-term, it would be effectively cut off from the zones of security and settlement unilaterally established by Israel. Moreover, the reoccupation of the West Bank and Gaza, as well as the systematic demolition of anything that might embody the Palestinian Authority, have resulted in the fragmentation and partitioning of the Territories. The project to set up cantons within the West Bank and Gaza, which would constitute so many separate enclaves bereft of any kind of self-sufficiency, would complete the work of sapping the foundations of a Palestinian state.

Finally, the efforts made by Ariel Sharon to exclude Yasser Arafat from the political process, and therefore to demand a brand new Palestinian leadership, completes this strategy. By seeking to bring forward Palestinian politicians who lack national stature, the Israeli government hopes to hasten the process of Palestinian disintegration. With Arafat and centralized Palestinian power out of the way, the Israeli Right could revert to a long-standing plan whereby there would be a form of local autonomy within which each canton would depend on the power of Israel as a last resort. The goal of this strategy would be to retain control over the physical space without directly assuming the task of administering the Palestinian population.

There can now be no question at all that the resolution of the Palestinian-Israeli conflict requires the intervention of the international community. The European Community has the capacity to act as a balancing influence between the two contestants; what is more, it possesses the means to exert strong financial pressures, insofar as it backs the Palestinian Authority with financial support and has signed a treaty of association with Israel. However, given that for the time being the EU is powerless to act as a united force on the international scene, it is hardly likely to intervene in any decisive way. Failure on this issue would only serve to sharpen the difficulties the EU already has in formulating a common foreign policy. Even though the EU's representative has firmly condemned Israel's behavior in the Territories,[4] the European Union has agreed to no sanction whatever against the state of Israel. It encourages and supports reforms within the Palestinian Authority but is in no position to demand that the violence be stopped.

As for the United States, it is possible that with the conclusion of the war in Iraq, it will start a fresh initiative to resolve the Palestinian problem. The regional picture has changed considerably, bringing new guarantees of security to Israel, and the United States may find itself in a position to demand concessions from the Israelis. Nothing could be less certain, however, given the extent of Washington's unconditional support for Israel in the past. Under pressure, the two sides could begin a new cycle of negotiations and reach a political agreement. Nevertheless it is important to point out that the formation of a Palestinian "state" in a segment of the pre-1967 Territories could be reduced to a cosmetic formula that would set in stone Israel's past methods of domination and control. Ariel Sharon has taken skillful advantage of the international situation. By likening the attacks on Israeli soil to the one that destroyed the World Trade Center, and by comparing Yasser Arafat to Osama Bin Laden, the Israeli prime minister has convinced the American administration that the United States and Israel are standing side by side in the same fight. When the offensive against Baghdad was launched, Ariel Sharon made yet another comparison between the head of the Palestinian Authority and Saddam Hussein. He dwelt on the Iraqi regime's payment of cash to the families of Palestinian suicide bombers, which in fact was entirely channeled through the Iraqi nationalist Ba'ath Party and had nothing to do with the Palestinian Authority. For their part, the Palestinians hold out very little hope of an American intervention. The refusal of George W. Bush's administration to consider Yasser Arafat as a valid negotiating partner, and the dearth of any U.S. reaction to Israel's crackdown within the Territories, are very bad omens. What's more, the Palestinians are convinced that the U.S. war in Iraq was aimed at strengthening Israel's strategic superiority in the region. They are also afraid that Israel will take advantage of the world's current obsession with Iraq to intensify the crackdown, perpetuate its exactions against civilians, and even organize mass expulsions of West Bank Palestinians into Jordan.

In general the Palestinians are ill-prepared to begin a new phase in their relations with Israel. They can count on nobody abroad and are themselves greatly weakened. Many of them doubt the effectiveness of the armed struggle, without having any real alternative to suggest. The only hope of a change of course lies within Israeli society, not within Palestinian society. Even though the *refuzenik* movement seems to have petered out, a growing number of Israelis are uncomfortably aware that the conflict has reached a deep impasse. If the repression goes any further and if any more unbearable images of massacres appear on Tel Aviv TV screens, Israeli consciences may finally be awakened. But Israeli society is a mass of contradictions: though some elements of the Left would dearly love to disencumber the nation of the occupation, give up the settlements, and preserve the lives of soldiers and civilians, the population as a whole seems to agree with its politicians that Israel is fighting for its survival. The balance between these two tendencies is affected by many other things, and there is no telling what the outcome may be. For the time being, Israel will have to choose between the preservation of its Jewish character and the preservation of its democratic identity, given the increasing numbers of non-Jews who now have Israeli citizenship. The manner in which the Israeli state handles these questions will in part determine the future of its relations with its Arab neighbors. In terms of a settlement of the Middle East conflict and the integration of the Jewish state into its predominantly Arab environment, the Israelis will have to compensate for their principal element of structural inferiority, which is demographic. Because of this the Palestinians could even turn out to be Israel's principal allies when it comes to competing with the other countries of the region. In any event, to ensure its own survival Israel needs to build a real peace based on real reconciliation. Each new death in the present conflict carries the two sides a little farther away from that prospect, even though a solution is not only necessary but also unavoidable and, ultimately, the only rational outcome.

NOTES

CHAPTER ONE
The Palestinian Intifada: The Revolt against Israeli Occupation, 1987–1994

1. At that time, prisoners were grouped in Israeli prisons according to their political affiliations.

2. Today he is a member of the Palestinian legislative council.

3. After Iraq's invasion of Kuwait in August 1990 and Saddam Hussein's subsequent refusal to withdraw his troops, the United States led a coalition of European and Arab states in an offensive against Iraq.

4. Khalil al-Wazir, alias Abu Jihad, a founding member of Fatah, was the original head of the western bureau. He was assassinated in Tunis by the Israeli secret service on April 16, 1988, for his role as a coordinator of the Intifada.

5. The Jordanian authorities issued passports to West Bank residents. Between 1948 and 1967, the territory belonged to the Hashemite Kingdom. The Jordanian regime officially broke its administrative ties with the West Bank—specifically, it stopped paying the salaries of civil servants—in 1988. In doing so, it condoned the PLO as the sole legitimate representative body of the Palestinian people. However, even after that date any inhabitant of the West Bank could obtain a Jordanian passport.

6. Ze'ev Schiff and Ehud Ya'ari, *Intifada* (Paris: Stock, 1991), p. 71.

7. An Israeli investigation among Palestinian prisoners in the early stage of the Intifada revealed that their political mobilization was less a function of ideology than a reaction against repeated humiliations at the hands of the Israeli armed forces. Cf. Schiff and Ya'ari, *Intifada,* pp. 100–104.

8. Literally, "father of Lana." Once they have children, men and women are called "father" (Abu) or "mother" (Umm) followed by the first name of their eldest son. In the absence of a son, they use the first name of their eldest daughter.

9. On the question of women's place in the Intifada, see Rema Hammauri, "L'Intifada a-t-elle emancipé les femmes?" *Revue d'études palestiniennes* 51 (Spring 1994).

10. HAMA, the Arabic acronym for "Islamic Resistance Movement," is the political offshoot of the Muslim Brothers. Breaking with its traditional passive role, the aim of which was to Islamize society in order to give it the means for an effective struggle against Israel, the association of Muslim Brothers created Hamas as a political movement that could take a vital part in the Intifada. The founding charter of Hamas

made clear its objectives: to build an Islamic state in Palestine, and to wipe Israel off the map. Jews would be permitted to live within this Islamic state, with the status of a protected minority.

11. "Ahmed Tabuq Yattahaddath li-l-majallah-Alwan' Alwan," November 15, 1955, Jerusalem, p. 19.

CHAPTER TWO
Building Palestinian Autonomy, 1994–2000

1. Amira Hass notes that "During the post-Oslo period, one-fifth of the Gaza Strip was reserved for the use of half of 1 percent of its overall population." *Boire la mer à Gaza* (Paris: La Fabrique, 2001), p. 266.

2. Cf. Franck Debie and Sylvie Fouet, *La paix en miettes, Israel et la Palestine (1993–2000)* (Paris: PUF, 2001).

3. The Wye River Memorandum was signed on October 23, 1998. The Sharm-el-Sheikh accord, known as Wye II, was concluded on September 4, 1999.

4. The Cairo agreement (Oslo I) and the Taba agreement (Oslo II) made up the interim arrangements.

5. For a more detailed analysis of the absorption of the shebab of the Intifada by the Palestinian Authority, see Laetitia Bucaille, *Gaza, la violence et la paix* (Paris: Presse de Sciences, 1998), chap. 3.

6. *Zakat* means alms. Islam requires the faithful to contribute a fraction of their income to charity; committees then manage the funds and distribute them to the needy.

CHAPTER THREE
Fault Lines among the Palestinians

1. In July 2000 there was conflict between workers from Gaza and local people from Qalailya, a town on the northern edge of the West Bank near the Green Line. Seven men were injured and a number of houses burned down. These clashes illustrated the exasperation and racist feeling of West Bank people vis-à-vis their Gaza compatriots, who had come to the region to earn a salary working in Israel.

2. Anne Lesch, "Prelude to the Uprising in the Gaza Strip," *Journal of Palestinian Studies* 20, 1 (Autumn 1990): 3–4.

3. The wealthy quarter of Gaza City.

4. A quote from Mohammed, 33, a Hamas militant who works in Israel.

5. The destruction of activists' houses is a regular tactic of the Israeli Army. This punishes the entire family of those individuals it is looking for or has imprisoned.

6. See Bucaille, *Gaza,* p. 247.

7. See chapter 1 for his role as an organizer.

8. For an exact account of this event, see Schiff and Ya'ari, *Intifada,* pp. 73–74.

9. Following the directives of the NUC, set up during the uprising, the population of the Territories boycotted the payment of services provided by Israel. Immediately

after the formation of the Palestinian Authority, the Jewish state demanded a settlement of these unpaid bills.

10. See the minutes of a debate organized in London, March 2000, when Azmi al-Shuaybi introduced his account "Institutions palestiniennes: histoire d'une enquête," *Revue d'études palestiniennes* 25 (Fall 2000): 75–86.

11. Ibid.

12. For an analysis of the relations between Hamas and the Palestinian Authority, see Bucaille, *Gaza,* chap. 5.

CHAPTER FOUR
Palestine and Israel: The Impossible Divorce

1. Leila Farsakh, *Palestinian Employment in Israel 1967–1997: A Review* (Ramallah: MAS, 1998).

2. See Leila Farsakh, *The Implementation of Labor-Related Articles in the Protocol on Economic Relations between Israel and the PLO: A Critical Assessment* (Ramallah, MAS, 1999).

3. Figures obtained from the Palestinian Central Bureau of Statistics, at www.pcbs. org.laborforce.html.

4. Right to Work Law: Economic Rights under Military Occupation, Jerusalem, November 1999.

5. Leila Farsakh, "Palestinian Labor Flows to Israel: Land and Labor since Oslo and Beyond," an exposé delivered at a conference of the Middle East Studies Association, November 2001.

6. For this reason, many Palestinians claim to prefer the Likud to the socialist government.

7. Figures obtained from the Palestinian Labor Ministry.

8. The socialist government had set the limit at 35, taking the view that younger men were potential candidates for suicide missions.

9. The industrial zones are closed spaces close to Palestinian towns. The Erez industrial zone on the frontier between the Gaza Strip and Israel has about a hundred Israeli firms and about twenty belonging to Palestinians. It was created by the Labor government during the 1970s in an attempt to place the Palestinian workforce at the disposal of Israeli investors while keeping them outside Israeli territory.

10. The Israeli Civil Administration is essentially a military structure that governs the territories conquered in 1967.

11. The number of permits allotted to this category increased in the late 1990s. According to the Israeli Ministry of Defense, 31,000 businesspeople were using this card in early 2000. In their book *La paix en miettes,* Franck Debie and Sylvie Fouet mention 16,5000 permits given to Palestinian merchants.

12. In the West Bank the rate was 5.4 children per woman. These figures are furnished by Farsakh, Implementation, p. 85. Philippe Fargues gives an even higher

birthrate for the Gaza Strip—9.8 children per woman. See Philippe Fargues, "Demographie de guerre, demographie de paix," in *Proche-Orient: Les exigences de la paix,* ed. Ghassan Salame (Brussels: Complexe, 1994), p. 26.

13. Philippe Fagues, "Des cartes, dans quelle jeu?," *Revue d'études palestiniennes* 28, (Spring 2000).

14. Aurélie Bouhours, "Des tentes aux murs: du provisoire au durable? Espace et identité dans la bande de Gaza," ms., institut de géographie Louis-Papy, Bordeaux-III, September 2001.

15. As settled with the Israelis, in negotiations for the Paris economic agreement.

16. Figures supplied by the economic branch of the Office of the Coordinator of Government Activities in the Territories, which comes under the Israeli Ministry of Defense.

17. To put this in context, Palestinian trade with the exterior in 1998 totaled 530 million dollars in exports and 2,420 billion dollars in imports, 80 percent of both trade and deficit with Israel (figures provided by the Poste d'expansion économique, French Consul General, Jerusalem).

18. In January 1994 the Palestinian Authority signed a technical and economic accord with Egypt, which gave certain products preferential trading status. A second accord was concluded with Jordan in January 1995, drawing up a list of sixty products that would benefit from free trade conditions.

19. To cross into Jordan or Egypt, Palestinian vehicles must obtain a permit that lasts for only ten hours.

20. The defeat of Shimon Peres by Benyamin Netanyahu in spring 1996 was principally due to a sea-change in Israeli public opinion after a series of five fatal terrorist attacks.

21. *Le Monde,* February 23, 2001, pp. 1–2.

22. Estimate given by Sara Roy, drawn from official American sources in "Economic Deterioration in the Gaza Strip," *Middle East Report,* July–September 1996, p. 37.

23. For more detailed information, see Bucaille, *Gaza,* chap. 4.

CHAPTER FIVE
Part-timers of War: The Al-Aqsa Intifada, 2000–2002

1. There is a general dread that the bicycle seat might accidentally break a girl's hymen.

2. The advent of the Samaritans as a separate branch of Judaism dates from the sixth century before Christ. A community that today consists of only 350 people, the Samaritans live in the village of al-Tur, a few kilometers from Nablus. They are represented by their own MP in the Palestinian Legislative Council; they are allowed to sell alcohol, and they are credited with the power to cast spells or free people who have fallen victim to them.

3. Antoine Lahad was the head of the Lebanon militia, a surrogate force operating on behalf of Israel in South Lebanon. Ehud Barak made the decision to evacuate the zone, and now Syria is the only foreign presence in Lebanon.

4. This analysis is to be taken with a grain of salt, because there has actually been a sharp increase in the numbers of arrests among Palestinian minors since the outbreak of the al-Aqsa Intifada. An article in *Ha'aretz,* the left-wing Israeli daily—a translated version appeared in the *Courrier International* of May 17, 2001—shows that 350 Palestinians aged between twelve and eighteen were sent to prison during the first seven months of the al-Aqsa Intifada. With jail sentences of several months handed down for stone-throwing, these boys found themselves undergoing the cruelty of adults in Israeli jails. Since the start of the latest Intifada, Palestinian families' right to visit their relatives in jail has been suspended.

5. To borrow the expression of Anne Muxel, who has worked on the relationship between young people and politics in France.

6. Children's Defense International, an NGO, has established that 105 Palestinian minors were killed in the course of 2000. A third of these died of bullet wounds to the head, a third were hit in the chest, and the remainder perished from other injuries.

7. Yahya Ayache, known as "The Engineer," was considered the leading bomb-maker for Hamas. Singled out by the Israelis as the mastermind behind several shattering attacks within Israel, he was eliminated by the Israeli security services, who planted a bomb in his mobile phone in December 1995. His funeral cortège in Gaza was followed by a gigantic crowd, and his assassination brought an end to a truce that Hamas had respected for several months. The vengeance that a dissident Hamas cell inflicted on the Israelis was a savage one, with five bloody attacks in February and March 1996.

8. Communiqué signed by Hisham Ismail Hamed, November 11, 1994, and distributed in Gaza.

9. *Reporters without Borders* has investigated the phenomenon of journalists injured in the fighting since the outset of the al-Aqsa Intifada. They report that between September 2000 and December 2001, forty-five reporters were hit by bullets, all from the Israeli side. The figures quoted do not include other incidents, such as beatings of journalists by the army, or reporters struck by rubber bullets. Nor is the total of forty-five considered to be definitive.

10. This institution, which functioned with highly qualified staff, had already created the basis for a general survey of the Palestinian population and its economy.

11. *La croix,* March 4, 2002.

12. This account of the assault on Jenin is based on an articles by Anton Kapeliouk, *Le monde diplomatique,* May 2002, and by Amira Hass, *Ha'aretz,* April 22, 2002.

13. See Uri Blau, "Inhuman Conditions in Israeli Detention Camps," *Kol Ha'ir,* May 24, 2002.

14. Quoted by Sylvain Cypel, "Traiter le cancer palestinien à la chimio," *Le Monde,* September 3, 2002.

CONCLUSION

1. According to figures supplied by the Israeli Information Center for Human Rights in the Occupied Territories.

2. *Libération,* March 5, 2002.

3. *Le Monde,* January 2, 2003.

4. Jean Bretèche, the EU representative in the West Bank and the Gaza Strip, has declared: "According to the Geneva Convention, an occupying army is bound to supply the population with minimal educational and health services, along with adequate food. Strictly speaking, the circumstances call for this; but within the Palestinian Territories the Israeli Army does not assume any such responsibility. So we may wonder today if we are not doing the work that properly should be that of the Israeli Army, and consequently whether we are not in some measure the proxies of the Israeli government. What is more, it is unacceptable that Israel should place difficulties in our way, when we are doing the work it should be doing. Humanitarian workers are being held up indefinitely at airports, aid trucks are being obstructed." *Le Monde,* December 11, 2002.

INDEX